WHAT EVERY MAN NEEDS TO KNOW

The Glory is the Answer

REGGIE TRAVIS

What Every Man Needs to Know

Trilogy Christian Publishers

A Wholly Owned Subsidiary of Trinity Broadcasting Network

2442 Michelle Drive, Tustin, CA 92780

For information, address Trilogy Christian Publishing

Rights Department, 2442 Michelle Drive, Tustin, CA 92780.

Trilogy Christian Publishing/ TBN and colophon are trademarks of Trinity Broadcasting Network.

For information about special discounts for bulk purchases, please contact Trilogy Christian Publishing.

Trilogy Disclaimer: The views and content expressed in this book are those of the author and may not necessarily reflect the views and doctrine of Trilogy Christian Publishing or the Trinity Broadcasting Network.

10 9 8 7 6 5 4 3 2 1

Library of Congress Cataloging-in-Publication Data is available.

ISBN 979-8-89333-237-7

ISBN (ebook) 979-8-89333-238-4

PREFACE

Have you ever lost something? I mean, something valuable to you, that you thought could never be replaced or ever found again? Maybe it was an heirloom, a door of opportunity, a relationship, or a precious gift. Whatever the case, whether it was your fault or not, now it was hopelessly gone, and you really don't know how it happened. Every shred of restoration has grown cold and dwindled away, but one lonely ember of promise still stirs deep inside your heart, that maybe, just maybe one day, you might find what was lost. That is what this book is about.

This book was not written for biblical scholars or doctors of theology. Instead, it was written for the average man and woman, who are not interested in biblical hermeneutics, exegesis, or some long-forgotten archaic language, but want to know how we have gotten ourselves into the pickle that we are experiencing today. Whether you are a church-going Christian or a skeptic, this book will strip away the leaves of religion and human effort and open your eyes to God's wonderful plan for you and men everywhere.

Introduction

We have all come face to face with circumstances and situations in life where we have no answers. In our current social climate, if we turn to those in leadership for solutions, we often get fed a bunch of ineffective rhetorical placebos. We are handed over to more hopelessness. We are left with the usual puzzling question, why? That is the million-dollar answer every man, woman, and child wants to know.

There are thousands of how to books. They run the entire gamut of topics. There are as many self-help, how to fix it, and how to get wealth books as there are stars in the sky. Certainly, some of them have helped corporations operate more efficiently and inspired some private individuals to succeed, but, by and large, most of society is left unaffected. What's the solution?

TABLE OF CONTENTS

Chapter 1: *What's the Problem?*

THE ELEPHANT IN THE ROOM

This idiom refers to a serious problem or situation which is noticed or perceived by everyone, but not spoken about due to fear of awkwardness, inability to address the issue, or fear of embarrassment. So, what happens in these situations? Everyone in the room pretends like the big hairy creature with the long trunk, swaying back and forth in the corner, is not even there. They hope that no one points out that mass of pachyderm sucking up all the oxygen and taking up all the available space in the room. If they do, someone will be forced to answer unavoidable and unwanted questions, for which they may not have answers. This is a dilemma for the world and especially for the church.

The church, the collective body of believers who have accepted Jesus Christ as their Lord and Savior, was created by God. He placed the church (the collective gathering of believers) among men, in neighborhoods, in communities, and wherever people can be touched by the power of His presence. Those local churches have spiritual authority over the world, over every community, and neighborhood in which they are located. If those churches remain reticent and a silent voice on social and moral issues, they have become derelict of their responsibilities from God. If those churches have lost their salt (truth), lost their power (ability), and lost their light (glory), they have become a powerless social club, operating under the guise of a church.

Therefore, their neighborhoods and communities suffer with a lack of spiritual authority and covering from God. Their neighborhoods and communities are like their very own Garden of Eden. Like Adam in the garden, if churches have become devoid of healing power, devoid of wisdom, devoid of truth, devoid of signs, devoid of wonders, and devoid of God's lifegiving flow of glory, they are an elephant in the room. So, what are we to do? Repent and seek God afresh! Stop being mesmerized by swelling homiletical orations, impressed by elaborate liturgical ceremonies, and hypnotized by apologetic naysayers. Nothing that God has created for the benefit of the church has passed away. Most important of all, refuse to settle for anything short of the truth, and absolutely run from religion and all its trappings.

The Glory is a Garment

What the masses of humanity, typical Sunday churchgoers, and even most Christians don't realize is that man was created in God's image and likeness. I know that sounds just like the usual bunch of church speak, but I assure you it is not. Adam and Eve were created with all of God's attributes, His ability, authority, character, and personality. But the crowning piece of man's creation was the robe of light that emanated from within and completely covered them from head to toe with God's overflowing, eternal life and light. That statement just ruffled a lot of religious and theological feathers and that's a good thing. Also, it is a very important bit of information for the average man and woman not to be overlooked, because it could change their lives forever. It was this holy flame of fire which Adam received when God breathed into his nostrils after forming him out of the dust of the ground.

Genesis 2:7 NKJV

And the LORD God formed man of the dust of the ground, and breathed into his nostrils the breath of life; and man became a living being.

It was this garment of light that made them distinctly different than any other creature on the face of the earth or in heaven. Yes, you heard me correctly. Adam and Eve were covered with a garment of light just like their Creator.

Genesis 1:26-28 NKJV

Then God said, "Let Us make man in Our image, according to Our likeness; let them have dominion over the fish of the sea, over the birds of the air, and over the cattle, over all the earth and over every creeping thing that creeps on the earth." So God created man in His own image; in the image of God He created him; male and female He created them. Then God blessed them, and God said to them, "Be fruitful and multiply; fill the earth and subdue it; have dominion over the fish of the sea, over the birds of the air, and over every living thing that moves on the earth."

Psalms 104:1-4 NKJV

Bless the Lord, O my soul! O Lord my God, You are very great: You are clothed with honor and majesty, Who cover Yourself with light as with a garment, Who stretch out the heavens like a curtain. He lays the beams of His upper chambers in the waters, Who makes the clouds His chariot, Who walks on the wings of the wind, Who makes His angels spirits, His ministers a flame of fire.

When God created the heavens and the earth, everything was made to have some sort of flesh as a covering. In addition to their fleshly garment, much of God's creation had an extra outer coat of bark, thorns, scales, fur, or feathers used for a specific function, for protection, or for show.

1 Corinthians 15:38-41 NKJV

But God gives it a body as He pleases, and to each seed its own body. All flesh is not the same flesh, but there is one kind of flesh of men, another flesh of animals, another of fish, and another of birds. There are also celestial bodies and terrestrial bodies; but the glory of the celestial is one, and the glory of the terrestrial is another. There is one glory of the sun, another glory of the moon, and another glory of the stars; for one star differs from another star in glory.

To remain here on the earth, you must have a garment of natural flesh. If your natural body suit dies, you no longer have a license, parking permit, nor a green card to stay here on the planet. Your natural body is like a gravity suit to help you to remain here on earth.

Otherwise, your soul and spirit fly away. Yes, man was created with a fleshly garment of skin like much of the rest of God's creation, but with one unique difference. Man's outer garment was a suit of glory from God Himself. It covered his flesh from head to toe and emanated from within and was a signature stamp of God's presence to all the animals and creation that God was with this man and flowing out of him. I did not say he was God. He was a part of God's family and a reflection of God's image and likeness that was set here on the earth. I know this revelation has shaken a bunch of your religious Legos, but just take a chill pill and before too long, your blood pressure will level out.

Paradise Lost

Here's the skinny. We all are familiar with the story of Adam and Eve in the garden and how they had eaten the fruit from the tree of the knowledge of good and evil which God had warned them not to eat, because they would die....

Genesis 2:15-17 NKJV

Then the Lord God took the man and put him in the garden of Eden to tend and keep it.

And the Lord God commanded the man, saying, "Of every tree of the garden you may freely eat; but of the tree of the knowledge of good and evil you shall not eat, for in the day that you eat of it you shall surely die."

Part of God's great love was to give a free will to His created beings. So instead of obeying God's words, they chose to believe the lies of the serpent in the garden.

Genesis 3:1-6 NKJV

Now the serpent was more cunning than any beast of the field which the LORD God had made. And he said to the woman, "Has God indeed said, 'You shall not eat of every tree of the garden'?" And the woman said to the serpent, "We may eat the fruit of the trees of the garden; but of the fruit of the tree which is in the midst of the garden, God has said, 'You shall not eat it, nor shall you touch it, lest you die.'"

Then the serpent said to the woman, "You will not surely die. For God knows that in the day you eat of it your eyes will be opened, and you will be like God, knowing good and evil." So when the woman saw that the tree was good for food, that it was pleasant to the eyes, and a tree desirable to make one wise, she took of its fruit and ate. She also gave to her husband with her, and he ate.

As a result of believing these lies, their eyes were opened. They saw that they were naked. They knew it and so did everything else. Now that their eyes were uncovered, they became aware that they were now without their glory covering (garment). This would be a better translation of this scripture. They had lost something. So, what did they do? To make up for their loss, they covered themselves with leaves.

Genesis 3:7-11 NKJV

Then the eyes of both of them were opened, and they knew that they were naked; and they sewed fig leaves together and made themselves coverings. And they heard the sound of the LORD God walking in the garden in the cool of the day, and Adam and his wife hid themselves from the presence of the LORD God among the trees of the garden. Then the LORD God called to Adam and said to him, "Where are you?" So he said, "I heard Your voice in the garden, and I was afraid because I was naked; and I hid myself." And He said, "Who told you that you were naked? Have you eaten from the tree of which I commanded you that you should not eat?"

What an absolute poor substitute for God's glory covering! Spiritually speaking, these leaves were a symbol of their attempt to replace the relationship and glory that they had lost, and at the same time satisfy their feelings of guilt and shame. Leaves were an attempt to make themselves feel comfortable, with themselves and others. But nothing can replace God's glory nor do His work like His anointing. The glory of God is the signature stamp of God's presence (His Holy Spirit) with you and me.

While attached to the trees, the leaves were fresh, lively, and vibrant, but as soon as they were plucked and used as a covering, they began to dry up and die. They were no longer connected to their source of life. Here is a spiritual truth. God's relationship and glory are our source of life. Where there is no relationship, there is no glory, and where there is no glory, things dry up and die. No man's feeble attempt to steady or stop this decay can succeed. The answer for spiritual dryness in the church is a fresh outpouring of God's Holy Ghost and fire. Question? Is the church in a season of dryness? Are you?

THE FRUIT OF THEIR DISOBEDIENCE

They were naked. They were uncovered and without their customary covering. They were exposed and completely without protection. They were ashamed. They were distressed and embarrassed from feelings of guilt, foolishness, and disgrace. As a result, they felt uncomfortable and awkward.

They were afraid. They were timid and fearful. They were scared, hesitant, unsure, unhappy, and disconnected from their original relationship with God and His family. They even hid themselves when He appeared in the garden (Genesis 3:10). They were now beginning to experience life without God's glory suit. They were left with just their natural human covering of skin and bones. They were no longer clothed in God's marvelous cloak of eternity, and to make things worse, their relationship with God was now changed.

Genesis 3:12-19 NKJV

Then the man said, "The woman whom You gave to be with me, she gave me of the tree, and I ate." And the LORD God said to the woman, "What is this you have done?" The woman said,

"The serpent deceived me, and I ate."

So the LORD God said to the serpent:

> *"Because you have done this,*
> *You are cursed more than all cattle,*
> *And more than every beast of the field;*
> *On your belly you shall go,*
> *And you shall eat dust*
> *All the days of your life.*
> *And I will put enmity*

Between you and the woman,
And between your seed and her Seed;
He shall bruise your head,
And you shall bruise His heel."
To the woman He said:

> *"I will greatly multiply your sorrow and your conception;*
> *In pain you shall bring forth children;*
> *Your desire shall be for your husband,*
> *And he shall rule over you."*

Then to Adam He said, "Because you have heeded the voice of your wife, and have eaten from the tree of which I commanded you, saying, 'You shall not eat of it':

> *"Cursed is the ground for your sake;*
> *In toil you shall eat of it*
> *All the days of your life.*
> *Both thorns and thistles it shall bring forth for you,*
> *And you shall eat the herb of the field.*
> *In the sweat of your face you shall eat bread*
> *Till you return to the ground,*
> *For out of it you were taken;*
> *For dust you are,*
> *And to dust you shall return."*

God put them out of the garden. He knew if they ate from the tree of life in their fallen state, they would remain in that condition forever. They would never die and would live separated from Him and without His glory covering throughout eternity.

But God, in His mercy, had a redemption plan. He shed blood and clothed them with a temporary covering until their relationship could be mended and His glory could be restored to them.

Genesis 3:21-24 NKJV

Also for Adam and his wife the LORD God made tunics of skin, and clothed them. Then the LORD God said,

"Behold, the man has become like one of Us, to know good and evil. And now, lest he put out his hand and take also of the tree of life, and eat, and live forever"— therefore the LORD God sent him out of the garden of Eden to till the ground from which he was taken. So He drove out the man; and He placed cherubim at the east of the garden of Eden, and the flaming sword to turned every way to keep the way of the tree of life.

Though man was driven from the garden, when God shed blood and covered them with skins, it was a sign of things to come. Throughout the Bible, God gives us hidden clues, little glimpses, and subtle hints to His plan of restoration for man.

Chapter 2: *Choose Wisely*

THE BLUE PILL OR THE RED PILL?

This is a reference to a popular 1999 action movie where two different realities could be experienced depending on which color pill you swallowed. In like manner, Adam and Eve had to metaphorically make a choice of whose words to swallow (believe), God's or the serpent's. They could have chosen a life with God's robe of light or a life with just a robe of flesh. They were deceived by the serpent and didn't make the right choice, and mankind has suffered with the consequences of sin ever since.

The Hebrew words for a robe of light (אוֹר) and a robe of skin (עוֹר) are spelled differently but they are pronounced the same (ore), but they lead to two different realities (lives, characters, abilities, and authorities).

Now the works of the robe of flesh are manifest which are these: adultery, fornication, uncleanness, lasciviousness, idolatry, witchcraft, hatred, variance, emulations, wrath, strife, seditions, heresies, envying, murder, drunkenness, and reveling (Galatians 5:19-21). On the other hand, the fruit (work) of the Spirit (God's glory suit) is love, joy, peace, patience, kindness, goodness, and faithfulness (Galatians 5:22 NKJV).

So, the truth of the matter is this: without a God-connection and robe of glory, man was doomed to suffer the ills and weaknesses of the robe of the flesh. Hence, today we are repeatedly crushed by the accusations of racism, deviant lifestyles, lies, Machiavellian politics, plagues (man-made or otherwise), and school shootings. Who will save us from ourselves?

It may seem like a hopeless situation for Adam and mankind due to his errant choice, but we have a great promise of hope and good news because what was lost in Adam is fully restored in Jesus.

Getting to the Root

Anyone who has planted a flower bed or any type of garden knows sometimes it can be hard work. It is labor intensive, requires diligence, patience, and attentiveness. On the other hand, it can be quite beautiful and rewarding to reap the fruits of your labor. An experienced gardener knows the ruination of all his hard cultivation work is weeds. If he is to be successful, he must be vigilant in eliminating any weeds that might choke out his plantings. Weeds are everywhere; that is the nature of most soils. To be rid of them, he must either pull them up from the root or kill their root. The root that is buried under ground is the source of the weed problem, not the part that is visible to us above ground.

Likewise, the root cause of the ills of man is not what we can see, it's what we can't see, hidden below the surface. A root cause is an initiating source of a chain of events producing results, either good or bad. The root cause of man's ills stems from Adam and Eve eating from a tree in the garden whose root was death and whose fruit produced a poisonous awareness of the knowledge of good and evil.

Genesis 3:1-3 NKJV

Now the serpent was more cunning than any beast of the field which the Lord God had made. And he said to the woman, "Has God indeed said, 'You shall not eat of every tree of the garden'?" And the woman said to the serpent, "We may eat the fruit of the trees of the garden; but of the fruit of the tree which is in the midst of the garden, God has said, 'You shall not eat it, nor shall you touch it, lest you die.'" This act of disobedience broke their relationship with God and choked off the flow of His robe of glory to them. From that moment, their lives began to experience the sap of death flowing through that tree. Now that Adam was devoid of his garment of glory, he was left with the toil and sweat of his hands to cultivate the garden. Now, in addition, he would have the daily task of weeding out the thorns and thistles.

Genesis 3:17-19 NKJV

Then to Adam He said, "Because you have heeded the voice of your wife, and have eaten from the tree of which I commanded you, saying, 'You shall not eat of it':
"Cursed is the ground for your sake;
In toil you shall eat of it
All the days of your life.
Both thorns and thistles it shall bring forth for you,
And you shall eat the herb of the field.
In the sweat of your face you shall eat bread
Till you return to the ground,
For out of it you were taken,
for dust you are,
And to dust you shall return."

How did he do it before? Why, he simply spoke to things just like his Creator God.

Mark 11:12-24 NKJV

Now the next day, when they had come out from Bethany, He was hungry. And seeing from afar a fig tree having leaves, He went to see if perhaps He would find something on it. When He came to it, He found nothing but leaves, for it was not the season for figs. In response Jesus said to it, "Let no one eat fruit from you ever again." And His disciples heard it.

So they came to Jerusalem. Then Jesus went into the temple and began to drive out those who bought and sold in the temple, and overturned the tables of the money changers and the seats of those who sold doves. And He would not allow anyone to carry wares through the temple. Then He taught, saying to them, "Is it not written, 'My house shall be called a house of prayer for all nations'? But you have made it a 'den of thieves.'" And the scribes and chief priests heard it and sought how they might destroy Him; for they feared Him, because all the people were astonished at His teaching. When evening had come, He went out of the city.

Now in the morning, as they passed by, they saw the fig tree dried up from the roots. And Peter, remembering, said to Him, "Rabbi, look! The fig tree which You cursed has withered away." So Jesus answered and said to them, "Have faith in God. For assuredly, I say to you, whoever says to this mountain, 'Be removed and be cast into the sea,' and does not doubt in his heart, but believes that those things he says will be done, he will have whatever he says. Therefore I say to you, whatever things you ask when you pray, believe that you receive them, and you will have them.

Consequences and Man's Fix

Every wise person knows that life's journey is a series of choices. The book of Proverbs admonishes us to follow wisdom and seek to do good, which has a promise of blessing.

Proverbs 3:1-10 NKJV

My son, do not forget my law, But let your heart keep my commands; For length of days and long life And peace they will add to you. Let not mercy and truth forsake you; Bind them around your neck, Write them on the tablet of your heart, And so find favor and high esteem In the sight of God and man. Trust in the Lord with all your heart, And lean not on your own understanding; In all your ways acknowledge Him, And He shall direct your paths.

Do not be wise in your own eyes; Fear the Lord and depart from evil. It will be health to your flesh, And strength to your bones. Honor the Lord with your possessions, And with the firstfruits of all your increase; So your barns will be filled with plenty, And your vats will overflow with new wine.

No man or woman born into this world intends to go astray or do that which is evil, but the root of that tree of death takes advantage of the weakness of the flesh. A man may spend his whole life doing good, but some evil, some sickness, or some disease befalls him. That's not fair! Is it? The tree that Adam and Eve ate from in the garden had a root of death and produced an experience of both good and bad (sweet and bitter). From the moment they ate that fruit, they slipped from the hands of God's glory into the reality of experiencing some good and some bad. That was the nature of the flesh life without the overflowing presence of God. This reality can easily be seen in Adam and Eve's first fruits, their sons Cain and Abel. One of the sons did good and one did wickedness. Thanks be to God that He would rescue man from this sad state into which he had fallen.

Because of the poisonous sap of the tree of the knowledge of good and evil, man has descended into lowly circumstances and his solutions are even lower. Man's answer for shootings is gun control, his answer for deviant lifestyles is inclusion, and his answer for social justice is protest or anarchy. The trouble with these human Band-Aids is that they don't address the underlying root cause in society. Don't be deceived for one minute longer; no legislation, no peace conference, or community action talk group will solve the problem. It is a spiritual (glory) issue and can't be solved with fleshly solutions. It is a poison and sickness of the human heart, which can only be healed by a blood transfusion from God. This was accomplished for man by the work of the cross, which all are invited to accept by faith. Will you receive that sacrifice today?

CHRONICLES

To be, or not to be clothed in God's marvelous invisible glory is a choice in life that every man and woman on the face of the earth must make at some point of their existence. It is the same crossroads that Adam and Eve faced in the garden. A man's life will speak loudly about whether his choice was wise or foolish. One thing is sure, your life will chronicle which spiritual path or reality you have taken. A chronicle is a history or record of events that have occurred over time.

The fruit of a man's lips, his words, will also chronicle his path in life. It can be compared to a man blowing a trumpet. That man can herald the events of his life, whether good or bad. A man covered with God's glory will speak of God's constant goodness. On the other hand, a man without that covering will rehearse his troubles, his sickness, his fear, his anger, and bitterness over and over, ad nauseam. Good or bad, the report of your lips has a direct bearing on your future direction and future success or failure.

James 3:3-6 NKJV

Indeed, we put bits in horses' mouths that they may obey us, and we turn their whole body. Look also at ships: although they are so large and are driven by fierce winds, they are turned by a very small rudder wherever the pilot desires. Even so the tongue is a little member and boasts great things. See how great a forest a little fire kindles! And the tongue is a fire, a world of iniquity. The tongue is so set among our members that it defiles the whole body, and sets on fire the course of nature; and it is set on fire by hell.

In short, the words of our mouth always chronicle the garment in which we are clothed, whether it is a robe of light or a robe of flesh. This wellspring of words emanates from a man's soul and spirit and is a testimony of his stance in life.

From the very moment a man chooses to be clothed (baptized in the Holy Ghost and fire), he becomes a walking, breathing testimony of God's goodness. Like the disciples in the book of Acts, there will be an account or record of situations in which God has used them personally to bring His power and grace to help others. They can't help but be witnesses.

Mark 16:15-18 NKJV

And He said to them, "Go into all the world and preach the gospel to every creature. He who believes and is baptized will be saved; but he who does not believe will be condemned. And these signs will follow those who believe: In My name they will cast out demons; they will speak with new tongues; they will take up serpents; and if they drink anything deadly, it will by no means hurt them; they will lay hands on the sick, and they will recover."

These Scriptures say that signs and wonders will follow those who believe and are baptized. Sure, some of the above signs seem a little cuckoo and dangerous, especially the way that some men interpret them today. By no means is God a tempter. God's Grace and Power are limitless. So, don't put Him in a religious box. Besides those listed above, He continuously performs all kinds of miracles today. Make a choice to be saturated with the Holy Ghost so that you might bring God's Grace to your neighbor. Choose wisely.

Chapter 3: *Are You a Code Breaker*

CHOOSE THE RIGHT FREQUENCY

There are two realms of reality: the natural and the spiritual. It is impossible to understand the spiritual realm with the natural mind or intellect. A man may be a trained biblical scholar, but without being born again he will produce works of natural conjecture. The scriptures encourage us to have the mind of Christ. In other words, a man should have a mind baptized and covered with God's anointing. If he does, there are no foolish statements such as: you never know what God is going to do, God works in mysterious ways, God needed another angel, or well, it must be God's will.

You must understand that the spiritual and natural are like two different radio frequencies. Without God's Spirit, you can't tune in, hear, understand, or even get a glimpse into God's kingdom. At this point, men usually make up speculations or assumptions. Jesus explains this spiritual truth to a biblical scholar named Nicodemus.

John 3:1-17 NKJV

There was a man of the Pharisees named Nicodemus, a ruler of the Jews. This man came to Jesus by night and said to Him, "Rabbi, we know that You are a teacher come from God; for no one can do these signs that You do unless God is with him." Jesus answered and said to him, "Most assuredly, I say to you,

*unless one is born again, he cannot see the kingdom of God."
Nicodemus said to Him, "How can a man be born when he is
old? Can he enter a second time into his mother's womb and be
born?"*

*Jesus answered, "Most assuredly, I say to you, unless one is born
of water and the Spirit, he cannot enter the kingdom of God.
That which is born of the flesh is flesh, and that which is born of
the Spirit is spirit. Do not marvel that I said to you, 'You must
be born again.' The wind blows where it wishes, and you hear
the sound of it, but cannot tell where it comes from and where
it goes. So is everyone who is born of the Spirit." Nicodemus
answered and said to Him, "How can these things be?"*

*Jesus answered and said to him, "Are you the teacher of Israel,
and do not know these things? Most assuredly, I say to you, We
speak what We know and testify what We have seen, and you
do not receive Our witness. If I have told you earthly things and
you do not believe, how will you believe if I tell you heavenly
things?*

*No one has ascended to heaven but He who came down from
heaven, that is, the Son of Man who is in heaven.*

*And as Moses lifted up the serpent in the wilderness,
even so must the Son of Man be lifted up, that whoever
believes in Him should not perish but have eternal life.*

*For God so loved the world that He gave His only begotten
Son, that whoever believes in Him should not perish but have
everlasting life.*

*For God did not send His Son into the world to condemn the
world, but that the world through Him might be saved.*

My friend, whether you know it or not, God is constantly trying to talk and have fellowship with you, but you need to tune in to His spiritual frequency.

I attended college at a major university in the western part of Virginia. During my freshman year, I met an electrical engineering student that everyone called Right-On Royster. He lived on the fourth floor of a dormitory adjacent to one of the large dining halls where he and most of his friends ate lunch. He had two six feet tall speakers, which he had built, in his room. It was not uncommon for Right-On to throw open his dorm windows during lunch and blast music across that quadrant of the campus. During the spring of that year, he became emboldened. Right-On decided to hijack the broadband signal and frequency of the campus radio station. At this point, from his dorm room, he was broadcasting all over the county and beyond without a license.

It was not long before FCC and FBI officials arrived at his dorm room on the fourth floor. Right-On, howbeit illegal, tapped into something he knew was all around us. Though the radio frequency was unseen, he knew enough electronically to not just tune the station on his stereo, but steal the signal. I don't recommend following his example because it will not end well for you. In like manner, God is omnipresent, all around us, and He is just waiting for you to tap into the frequency of His goodness. It is impossible without the help of His Spirit. This is the reason why many people can't understand the Bible. Will you be bold enough to seek after God's frequency today? It is found by receiving the finished work of Jesus on the cross in your heart and being baptized in His Spirit.

DIGGING OUT HIDDEN SECRETS

From ages gone by, men everywhere, the prophets, and the angels have desired to know when, where, and how God's plan to restore man would occur. This mystery has been hidden in God since the beginning of time.

1 Peter 1:9-12 NKJV

Of this salvation the prophets have inquired and searched carefully, who prophesied of the grace that would come to you, searching what, or what manner of time, the Spirit of Christ who was in them was indicating when He testified beforehand the sufferings of Christ and the glories that would follow. To them it was revealed that, not to themselves, but to us they were ministering the things which now have been reported to you through those who have preached the gospel to you by the Holy Spirit sent from heaven--things which angels desire to look into.

Throughout the scriptures, men wanted to know when the kingdom of God would appear, and the sad thing is that many are still waiting. During much of the writing of the New Testament, the nation of Israel was under the hand of Roman rule. The Israeli people were praying and waiting for the Messiah to come conquer Rome, so that their nation would rule that part of the world once again. Both the Pharisees and the disciples asked Jesus concerning the kingdom and when it would come.

Luke 17:20-24 NKJ

Now when He was asked by the Pharisees when the kingdom of God would come, He answered them and said, "The kingdom of God does not come with observation; nor will they say, 'See here!' or 'See there!' For indeed, the kingdom of God is within you." Then He said to the disciples, "The days will come when you will desire to see one of the days of the Son of Man, and you will not see it. And they will say to you, 'Look here!' or 'Look there!' Do not go after them or follow them. For as the lightning that flashes out of one part under heaven shines to the other part under heaven, so also the Son of Man will be in His day."

Acts 1:6-7 NKJV

Therefore, when they had come together, they asked Him, saying, "Lord, will You at this time restore the kingdom to Israel?" And He said to them, "It is not for you to know times or seasons which the Father has put in His own authority."

This is commonly known as liberation ideology. Jesus answered this question by saying that seasons and times are in God's hands, and it should not be their concern. What their focus should be on is the power and outpouring of the Holy Spirit, because it was the fulfillment of the restoration of man's glory (Acts 1:8). In that moment of time, His disciples just could not see it. Men had no idea what great treasure was awaiting them. They, like many people today, don't realize that they have entered the door of God's kingdom when they accept the sacrifice that Jesus made for them on Calvary. Because many believers are not aware of this truth, they live far below God's best for them. Until after the dispensation of the sacrifice of Jesus on the cross, the plan of man's restoration remained hidden.

Colossians 1:25-27 NKJV

... of which I became a minister according to the stewardship from God which was given to me for you, to fulfill the word of God, the mystery which has been hidden from ages and from generations, but now has been revealed to His saints. To them God willed to make known what are the riches of the glory of this mystery among the Gentiles: which is Christ in you, the hope of glory. I have become its servant by the commission God gave me to present to you the word of God in its fullness—the mystery that has been kept hidden for ages and generations, but is now disclosed to the Lord's people. To them God has chosen to make known among the Gentiles the glorious riches of this mystery, which is Christ in you, the hope of glory.

Now and then, small bits and pieces of God's spiritual puzzle were revealed through His holy prophets. Hunger and thirst for the things (the restoration) of God is the key that opens the door to a God-filled life.

Matthew 5:6 NKJV

Blessed are those who hunger and thirst for righteousness, For they shall be filled.

A man's hunger will cause him to seek God and aggressively search for and dig out God's truths. In doing so, he realizes the exceeding great value of the treasure that he has found and makes it his own.

Matthew 13:44-45 NKJV

"Again, the kingdom of heaven is like treasure hidden in a field, which a man found and hid; and for joy over it he goes and sells all that he has and buys that field.

"Again, the kingdom of heaven is like a merchant seeking beautiful pearls.

God's plans are hidden in plain sight for all to see. Throughout the Bible, there are subtle clues of God's plans to restore His lost relationship with man and the glory they once shared. God, in His infinite wisdom, gives us glimpses of just how He plans to do this thing. Yes, even the prophets of old searched the scriptures diligently to decipher God's plan of redemption and His restoration code.

Why do I refer to God's plan as a code? The answer is because every code has certain elements and when these elements are combined they form a picture. Like a key, the picture can be used to unlock a mystery.

To get a true picture of God's plan, what threads of code should we be looking for in the scriptures? The answers can be found in the encounter in the Garden of Eden: selfishness; deception; separation; fear and shame; remorse; shedding of blood; forgiveness; restoration.

Luke 15:11-32
(paraphrased)

A certain man had two sons and the younger of them, being selfishly deceived, asked for his portion of the inheritance before the appointed time. While separated from his father's family, he spent his entire substance on riotous living. Soon, a famine engulfed the land and he found himself in dire straits and without his father's security. He hired himself into a shameful and hopeless condition until he came to his senses and remembered the goodness in his father's household. His feelings of remorse led him to return to a waiting father who received him with joy and forgiveness. Then his father did something very special: he shed covenant blood (killed the fatted calf) and covered his young son with a robe of righteous glory and put a ring on his finger. In doing so, he restored their relationship and everything the son had lost.

There are numerous parables, prophecies, and stories in the Bible that have similar hidden codes to God's wonderful wisdom. They are there for our discovery and God's glory. Why? Because every family on the face of the earth has suffered through some sort of broken relationship or loss, some hurt, or a seemingly hopeless situation, where God's glory can flood in and make the difference in their lives.

THE POWER OF THE CODE

The hidden code of God is the mystery of Jesus Christ and His purpose. The Lord, in His wisdom, covered this plan with His hands until the time was right. The death, burial, and resurrection of Jesus was the key that unlocked the unsearchable riches of God's glory for all mankind. The purpose was to allow men to believe (have fellowship and communion with) this mystery once it was revealed. In doing so, this mystery seed would produce a power and strength in a man's heart that would give him access to an overflowing God life. Also, the revelation of this glorious code of mystery towards mankind was a wonderful display of God's manifold wisdom before all the heavenly principalities and powers.

Ephesians 3:1-21 NKJV

For this reason I, Paul, the prisoner of Christ Jesus for you Gentiles--if indeed you have heard of the dispensation of the grace of God which was given to me for you, how that by revelation He made known to me the mystery (as I have briefly written already, by which, when you read, you may understand my knowledge in the mystery of Christ), which in other ages was not made known to the sons of men, as it has now been revealed by the Spirit to His holy apostles and prophets: that the Gentiles should be fellow heirs, of the same body, and partakers of His promise in Christ through the gospel, of which I became a minister according to the gift of the grace of God given to me by the effective working of His power. To me, who am less than the least of all the saints, this grace was given, that I should preach among the Gentiles the unsearchable riches of Christ, and to make all see what is the fellowship of the mystery, which from the beginning of the ages has been hidden in God who created all things through Jesus Christ; to the intent that now the manifold wisdom of God might be made known by the church to the principalities and powers in the heavenly places, according to the eternal purpose which He accomplished in Christ Jesus our Lord, in whom we have boldness and access with confidence through faith in Him.

Therefore I ask that you do not lose heart at my tribulations for you, which is your glory. For this reason I bow my knees to the Father of our Lord Jesus Christ, from whom the whole family in heaven and earth is named, that He would grant you, according to the riches of His glory, to be strengthened with might through His Spirit in the inner man, that Christ may dwell in your hearts through faith; that you, being rooted and grounded in love, may be able to comprehend with all the saints what is the width and length and depth and height--to know the love of Christ which passes knowledge; that you may be filled with all the fullness of God. Now to Him who is able to do exceedingly abundantly above all that we ask or think, according to the power that works in us, to Him be glory in the church by Christ Jesus to all generations, forever and ever. Amen.

Until now, I have not mentioned several other important aspects of man's restoration story. First, it is the fact that the Bible is a book of spiritual truth, history, prophecy, intrigue, and mystery. Secondly, it is a chronology of war, strategy, and espionage. This war has been waged for ages between the kingdom of Almighty God and that of Satan. It has been a continuous chess match between the forces of light and darkness for the hearts and souls of men. Third, it is a historical account of God's covenant relationship with man, which we first see glimpses of in the Garden of Eden, when God shed the blood of an animal to cover man's nakedness.

Genesis 3:21 NKJV

Also for Adam and his wife the Lord God made tunics of skin, and clothed them.

This is a conflict in which God declared victory over Satan in the garden. It was finished and secured by the death, burial, and resurrection of Jesus.

Genesis 3:14-15 NKJV

So the Lord God said to the serpent: "Because you have done this, You are cursed more than all cattle, And more than every beast of the field; On your belly you shall go, And you shall eat dust All the days of your life. And I will put enmity Between you and the woman, And between your seed and her Seed; He shall bruise your head, And you shall bruise His heel."

It is the glory of God to conceal a thing, but the honor of kings to search out a matter. The secret things belong to God, but the things revealed belong to us and our children, that we might prosper. Early on, God made known that He would not hide parts of His plans from righteous men like Abraham, but those without a connection with God would remain clueless. To accomplish this promise, God gave us the gift of the prophets and their ministry. The prophets passed on insight into God's hidden codes of redemption. In God's wisdom, He knew if His plan was fully revealed too soon, man would somehow corrupt the results. Not to mention, there is an adversary, Satan, whose job is to steal, kill, and destroy. In His infinite wisdom, God made sure His hidden biblical code was unbreakable by His enemy.

In a similar fashion, the United States government employed a special group of Marines during World War II. These special liaisons were known as the "Navajo Code Talkers." They received and transmitted sensitive information right in the enemy's face from 1942 to 1945. These Navajo Native American Marines developed their own special code of communication from their complex unwritten native language. Though their code messages were heard by the enemy Axis Powers (Germany, Italy, and Japan), they remained unbreakable and made our war efforts successful.

Like the prophets of God, the Navajo Code Talkers had a language that was exclusively cultural and spiritually based in the Navajo tribal kingdom, of which the Axis Powers had no knowledge, familiarity, or access. The enemies of Almighty God also have no knowledge, familiarity, nor access to righteousness, truth, or light. So, even today, God's words remain an unbreakable code of mystery to His adversaries, but an understandable source of wisdom and guidance to God's prophets and His people.

Unlocking the Kingdom

There are thousands of large corporate buildings all over the face of the earth and just as many CEOs of those companies. Those corporate giants have the authority to make decisions, to determine company policy and direction, but there is someone else with the ability to affect more things at the ground level so that an atmosphere is created to get things done. That individual is the most inconspicuous of all the employees in the company, and usually does their work in the background. He is the company janitor. He has the keys to unlock every door, set the climate controls, turn the lights on or off, clean up messes, and make things comfortable. The janitor's repertoire of skills makes him indispensable. Though somewhat invisible in the company hierarchy, he possesses the keys that allow the everyday operation of those businesses to flow smoothly. So it is with a man who has allowed his life to be saturated with God's Spirit; he has grace to unlock the kingdom of God for himself and those around him.

2 Corinthians 4:7 NKJV

But we have this treasure in earthen vessels, that the excellence of the power may be of God and not of us.

The Swiss Army Knife of God

The Swiss Army knife is a renowned multi-tooled knife that gained popularity during WWII. It usually has several knife blades, a can opener, a screwdriver, and a pair of scissors. It is the perfect functional tool to handle everyday problems. No man should be without one. Likewise, the gifts of the Holy Spirit are given to men to deal with everyday problems. To be sure, the motivation behind the use of these gifts is God's love. No, they have not passed away or become obsolete, as some would claim. For our benefit, God would not have us remain ignorant concerning their purpose for our lives. They are spiritual, not physical, gifts. A man covered with God's glory has access to the wonderful gifts of the Holy Ghost as his spiritual tools. He may need wisdom or knowledge to solve a mystery, he may need power for healing, he may need the gift of faith, or the working of miracles. In a manner of speaking, these gifts are keys that unlock the kingdom of God to bless men.

1 Corinthians 12:1-11 NKJV

Now concerning spiritual gifts, brethren, I do not want you to be ignorant: You know that you were Gentiles, carried away to these dumb idols, however you were led. Therefore I make known to you that no one speaking by the Spirit of God calls Jesus accursed, and no one can say that Jesus is Lord except by the Holy Spirit. There are diversities of gifts, but the same Spirit. There are differences of ministries, but the same Lord.

And there are diversities of activities, but it is the same God who works all in all. But the manifestation of the Spirit is given to each one for the profit of all: for to one is given the word of wisdom through the Spirit, to another the word of knowledge through the same Spirit, to another faith by the same Spirit, to another gifts of healings by the same Spirit, to another the working of miracles, to another prophecy, to another discerning of spirits, to another different kinds of tongues, to another the interpretation of tongues. But one and the same Spirit works all these things, distributing to each one individually as He wills.

Chapter 4: *The Glory Can Find You*

GOING AFTER THE LOST

People get lost or lose their way in life because of all kinds of reasons, most of which are not good. They get trapped, held up, broken, bruised, and wounded so badly that it is hard to return or ever trust again. Some people lose their way because they have been abused, tricked, stolen, offended, or are just plain rebellious. Whatever the reason, the Lord sent Jesus to give them a door (a chance) to come back and be whole again. God can hear the desperate cries of people just like the bleating cry of a little lost lamb. When He checks His inventory and finds that you are missing, He sends His glory to find you. Will you respond? Will you be clothed in God's glory so the lost can be found?

Luke 15:1-7 NKJV

Then all the tax collectors and the sinners drew near to Him to hear Him. And the Pharisees and scribes complained, saying, "This Man receives sinners and eats with them." So He spoke this parable to them, saying: "What man of you, having a hundred sheep, if he loses one of them, does not leave the ninety-nine in the wilderness, and go after the one which is lost until he finds it? And when he has found it, he lays it on his shoulders, rejoicing. And when he comes home, he calls together his friends and neighbors, saying to them, 'Rejoice with me, for I have found my sheep which was lost!' I say to you that likewise there will be more joy in heaven over one sinner who repents than over ninety-nine just persons who need no repentance.'"

Her Name was Terrie

We arrived in Myrtle Beach around 10:00 p.m. and we had just enough time for a snack before bed. While we discussed plans for the next day, our hosts hit us with bombshell news. They had become pastors of a new church in town and invited us to help get things started. Yes, we were familiar with that part of the plan, but the part we didn't know was a problem from the moment the words left their lips. First thing in the morning, they were planning for us to meet at the church for prayer and then go door to door witnessing. While our hosts were leaping with uncontrollable joy, the five of us were glancing at each other with a look of sly disdain or hidden disgust. I remember thinking sarcastically, "Ooh, I can hardly wait."

The next morning came entirely too soon. There we were, standing in a neighborhood of about 150 to 200 houses. I thought to myself, "Oh God! This is going to be a long day." There were eight of us, so we divided into four teams of two. My partner was the assistant pastor of their new church; his name was Vaughn. He didn't waste much time and politely asked me would I prefer praying or talking as we went door to door. My response was, "Praying," of course! Vaughn and I took the very first house and the rest of our team moved on.

As we approached the door, my first prayer was, "Lord, please don't let them have an aggressive dog in this house." Real spiritual, right? Vaughn rang the doorbell several times before anyone came to answer. Finally, the door opened about an inch and Vaughn began introducing us and explained that we were from a new church in the area. He went on to say that we were going through the neighborhood inviting people to attend one of our services. He asked, "What is your name" and she said it was Terrie. Finally, he asked, "Is there anyone in your house we can pray for?" Without saying a word, she closed the door. There was a rustling of a security chain, then the door swung wide open and standing there in front of us was a young African American woman about 23 years old.

Vaughn and I entered the house and the three of us sat down in separate chairs. I continued to pray softly as Vaughn gave her a brochure from the church. Up to this point, other than her name, she had not spoken a word. There was such an awkward and uneasy feeling in the atmosphere that I kept trying to loosen my collar. God! I wished that I was anywhere else but here. It didn't help that the woman sitting across from me had a body posture and demeanor that spoke loud and clear. Her body language and facial expressions changed from, "Why did I do this?" to "I wish I was somewhere else." At other times, it seemed as though she was indifferent to the whole situation. Then it happened. Vaughn asked her, "If you died today, do you know if you would go to heaven or hell?" I absolutely hate it when people in ministry ask that question. Seemingly unphased, Terrie sat there in silence with a mean mug facial expression. It seemed like an eternity. Then he asked if she would like to give her life to Jesus. Almost immediately, she said, "Yes." From my chair across the room, I blurted out, "No, you don't! You don't know what you are saying!" Her body language said, "no," but her lips said "yes." I was totally confused. Vaughn gave me a look that said, "Man, what are you doing?" I wanted to know if she really understood his question. She said, "Yes, I understand what he is asking me." We stood in the middle of the room to pray.

God is so faithful and good to us. As we began to pray, the presence of the Holy Spirit filled the room. It started as a whisper from somewhere deep inside of her but got louder and louder. Terrie began to shout over and over, "I'm free! I'm free! I'm free!" Suddenly, like a rocket, she began to run laps throughout the house. We were left standing there stunned with our mouths opened just watching her run. Finally exhausted, she stopped in front of us and began to cry. With great sobs of tears and remorse she said, "I didn't mean to kill that baby." By this time, Vaughn and I were in absolute and complete shock. She explained that she was babysitting for a friend. While driving to a nearby park to play, another driver ran through a red light and hit her car. The infant was killed in the accident and her ankle was shattered. But now, she said, "I'm free and my ankle that would not heal before after two operations is perfect." She began to jump up and down on her newly healed ankle.

We spent the better part of the next hour and a half answering her questions and praying with her. To our surprise, Terrie informed us that this was not her house. She was house-sitting and just like us arrived around 10:30 p.m. the night before. She went to bed broken and hopeless with the thought, "If things don't change tomorrow, I will go ahead with my suicide plans," but God, in His mercy, sent Vaughn and me to that house at the right time and by the power of His grace He saved her and changed her life forever. Terrie did attend those church services and remains a vital part of that congregation today. God is constantly looking to mend a broken relationship and restore a robe of glory to the lost, because that is the answer to every man's "Why?"

Today, we live in the world of the quick fix, the "I deserve it," the "I want it now," and the "something for nothing handout" culture. In the scriptures, we see that when the people had godly leadership to guide them, they had stability, peace, and righteous lives. When godly leadership was absent, every man did what was right in his own eyes, which always leads to a chaotic society. Under these circumstances, it is very easy for people, and even the church, to lose their spiritual compass. The church was established to be a beacon of hope and light in the community, but more importantly, it should be the epicenter of truth. If a lie is believed rather than the truth, the Holy Ghost (the spirit of truth) doesn't have liberty to operate. Here is a spiritual truth: if society is chaotic, the leadership has been ungodly, the church is powerless, and the sheep are weak and scattered.

It is a sad thing when sheep (Christians) are weak. They have accepted Jesus Christ as their Savior, but they remain powerless, timid, and hopeless, just like the rest of the world. The only difference is they go to church on Sundays. It is the word of truth and the spirit of truth that produces strong and victorious Christians full of faith and power. The difference between a strong Christian and a weak Christian is the spiritual food they eat. In other words, it is what a person believes in his heart and accepts as truth. If a believer is fed a bunch of religious ideas mixed with worldly idioms (unbelief), rather than truth, their Christian walk is stunted and weak.

God, in His mercy, is always sympathetic to the plight of men, no matter the circumstances. But know this, there are conditions to satisfy to get God's help. A heart of repentance and faith in the truth will unlock God's lovingkindness and glory every time. Without faith it is impossible to please God, but everyone that comes to God in faith must believe that He is a rewarder of those who seek Him.

Where there is no faith in the heart or atmosphere, there is no place for God to work. That is a sad situation, but unfortunately a very common occurrence.

A friend of mine asked me to pray for a man in his church. We visited the gentleman's home around 11:00 a.m. on Saturday morning. When we arrived, there were three people waiting for us, two lady relatives and a gentleman in a wheelchair. From what I was told, the rest of the family was at church preparing for the daughter's wedding. These were church going people, but something was missing. From the moment we walked in, I noticed that there was an absence of faith or expectancy in the atmosphere. I tried to ignore this spiritual vacuum, but that never works. So, I began to speak to them about the sacrifice of Jesus and the love of God, but they expressed absolutely no interest, nor was there an affirmative response from any of them. It was like plowing a field of concrete. I laid my hands on the gentleman several times and prayed for him in the name of Jesus, but to no avail. It was like they were not interested in the whole affair. They were in a sad and disappointing spiritual state. Yes, God's glory had found them, but they would not respond with a heart of faith. Will you?

HE'S GOT MY BACK

There was no one more disappointed than my friend and I as we left that gentleman in his wheelchair. So, to cheer me up, my friend offered to buy me lunch. I soon realized that it was my friend's faith that their family was leaning on, because they expressed none of their own. Over burgers and fries, we discussed our visit. He paused for a moment and with a look of bewilderment he asked, "Who was the man standing behind you?"

"What man?" I asked.

"The man in the corner," he said. Besides the gentleman in the wheelchair, we were the only men in the roo, that I saw. "What did he look like?" I asked.

His reply startled me. "He was covered from head to toe with fire and was just listening and watching. I got the impression that he was waiting for something to happen, like a signal or a word, but nothing happened. When we left, he left." Then my friend said, "What do I know, I've only been saved (born again) three weeks. I'm new at this, I thought this kind of thing happens all the time." Lord God! help our unbelief.

Your Glory Visited Me

Some years ago, I trained and worked as a volunteer for a prison fellowship ministry group. Over the weekend, we would visit different prisons and minister to the inmates. For three days, there would be a biblical teaching, praise and worship, and a time of interaction. On one occasion, we visited a maximum-security facility. The inmates there were serving thirty years to life sentences. They were incarcerated there for committing serious crimes. As soon as we arrived, our ministry team was escorted by armed guards through a series of check points and gates until we reached our meeting room. There were about thirty men that showed up. At first, there was a feeling of nervousness, but there was also a sense of expectation and hunger in those men. A few of them didn't know why they came, but when God is dealing with us, sometimes we are clueless. Over the course the weekend, the toughest man, the strongest wall, and the introverted man opened his heart, because the glory of God is genuine. On the last day, something special happened in that room that I don't think anyone there will ever forget.

Over the years, I have participated in several complex musical productions, with all the fancy lighting and musical arrangements, but this was different. It began like a whisper of wind. Like little children in Sunday School, all the inmates began to sing, "Jesus Loves Me." The presence of God's glory swept into that room in such a way that it was tangible. It was almost two or three minutes before I realized that I was standing and singing with my eyes closed. When I did open my eyes, all the inmates were either kneeling with hands raised in worship, bowed with their head to the ground, or lying prostrate on the floor singing with joyous tears of worship.

Suddenly but quietly, behind me, the door to the room was reverently opened and in stepped a prison official. Everyone was so absorbed in worship that very little attention was given to the newcomer in the room. That prison official, whom later I was told was the warden, stood quietly observing for about a minute and then something very special occurred. To everyone's surprise, the warden knelt in reverence to the glory of God's presence in that meeting room. The Lord has given us a promise to inhabit our praises and that is certainly what He did that day. The warden, the inmates, as well as our team, responded with praise and worship to the tangible presence of God, which no doubt affected the hearts of everyone in that room. My parting thoughts after that series of meetings were sobering. I thought to myself, "That was real church. What are we doing outside these prison walls? Unlike these men, we are free. Are we just playing church every Sunday?" God, visit us with Your presence.

Matthew 25:31-46 NKJV

"When the Son of Man comes in His glory, and all the holy angels with Him, then He will sit on the throne of His glory. All the nations will be gathered before Him, and He will separate them one from another, as a shepherd divides his sheep from the goats. And He will set the sheep on His right hand, but the goats on the left.

Then the King will say to those on His right hand, 'Come, you blessed of My Father, inherit the kingdom prepared for you from the foundation of the world: for I was hungry and you gave Me food; I was thirsty and you gave Me drink; I was a stranger and you took Me in; I was naked and you clothed Me; I was sick and you visited Me; I was in prison and you came to Me.' Then the righteous will answer Him, saying, 'Lord, when did we see You hungry and feed You, or thirsty and give You drink? When did we see You a stranger and take You in, or naked and clothe

You? Or when did we see You sick, or in prison, and come to You?' And the King will answer and say to them, 'Assuredly, I say to you, inasmuch as you did it to one of the least of these My brethren, you did it to Me.'

Then He will also say to those on the left hand, 'Depart from Me, you cursed, into the everlasting fire prepared for the devil and his angels: for I was hungry and you gave Me no food; I was thirsty and you gave Me no drink; I was a stranger and you did not take Me in, naked and you did not clothe Me, sick and in prison and you did not visit Me.' Then they also will answer Him, saying, 'Lord, when did we see You hungry or thirsty or a stranger or naked or sick or in prison, and did not minister to You?' Then He will answer them, saying, 'Assuredly, I say to you, inasmuch as you did not do it to one of the least of these, you did not do it to Me.'

And these will go away into everlasting punishment, but the righteous into eternal life."

GOD WILL ANSWER YOUR FAITH

God is not aloof from all the situations that we are experiencing. He has an ear and an eye on every individual. Don't ever get the idea that He doesn't care, because He does. He desperately wants to get involved in our lives, but He needs a door of invitation. No matter how extreme or intense your circumstance, God does not respond to tears, pain, or begging. God is moved by faith. Quite often, people get angry and blame God for things because they don't get an answer to their dilemma. Their anger shuts the door in God's face, so that they can't receive His blessing. Ignoring the laws of faith, they want God's help, but on their terms. Thinking their constant bleating will garner attention, they approach God with a whining and crying attitude, unaware that this approach will not cause God to move on their behalf.

It takes faith. Initially, the faith of repentance is the key that unlocks God's goodness. Repentance is the act of changing your heart and going in another direction. Faith is simply believing God's word over all the noise, believing through the storm, believing despite naysayers, and believing in the face of hopelessness. God is looking and listening for those who will believe and receive the finished work of Jesus and His words of truth. By His glory (the power of His Holy Spirit), He will search and find them wherever they are located. It is faith that pleases God and causes Him to run to your aid. It is faith that convinces Him that you believe that He exists and that He is a rewarder and promise keeper to all who diligently seek after Him. That very thing sets you apart from everyone else.

Hebrews 11:1-7 NKJV

Now faith is the substance of things hoped for, the evidence of things not seen. For by it the elders obtained a good testimony.

By faith we understand that the worlds were framed by the word of God, so that the things which are seen were not made of things which are visible.

By faith Abel offered to God a more excellent sacrifice than Cain, through which he obtained witness that he was righteous, God testifying of his gifts; and through it he being dead still speaks.

By faith Enoch was taken away so that he did not see death, "and was not found, because God had taken him"; for before he was taken he had this testimony, that he pleased God. But without faith it is impossible to please Him, for he who comes to God must believe that He is, and that He is a rewarder of those who diligently seek Him.

By faith Noah, being divinely warned of things not yet seen, moved with godly fear, prepared an ark for the saving of his household, by which he condemned the world and became heir of the righteousness which is according to faith.

Hebrews 11:30-40 NKJV

By faith the walls of Jericho fell down after they were encircled for seven days. By faith the harlot Rahab did not perish with those who did not believe, when she had received the spies with peace.

And what more shall I say? For the time would fail me to tell of Gideon and Barak and Samson and Jephthah, also of David and Samuel and the prophets: who through faith subdued kingdoms, worked righteousness, obtained promises, stopped the mouths of lions, quenched the violence of fire, escaped the edge of the sword, out of weakness were made strong, became valiant in battle, turned to flight the armies of the aliens. Women received their dead raised to life again.

Others were tortured, not accepting deliverance, that they might obtain a better resurrection. Still others had trial of mockings and scourgings, yes, and of chains and imprisonment. They were stoned, they were sawn in two, were tempted, were slain with the sword. They wandered about in sheepskins and goatskins, being destitute, afflicted, tormented— of whom the world was not worthy. They wandered in deserts and mountains, in dens and caves of the earth.

And all these, having obtained a good testimony through faith, did not receive the promise, God having provided something better for us, that they should not be made perfect apart from us.

Faith is a spiritual substance called believing, which is derived and created by your hope (an expectant imagination). It is a process that we as children are born with and learn to practice from birth, but as adults, it is corrupted by our worry, fear, doubt, and bad experiences. We call this daydreaming (making mental pictures from words). For children, imagination (make believe) and reality can be one and the same, so faith comes much easier to them. That is the very reason Jesus presented the gospel in parables (word pictures), so that people would have something on which to hang their expectations. It only takes childlike faith to please God. The glory of God can take that faith substance and create miracles. We call that process "believing" (a confident assurance).

A man or woman who chooses to believe God's words is like a beacon of light in a world of darkness. They are a stark contrast to an unbelieving world.

What they say and do is like a spiritual Bluetooth frequency which the Holy Spirit can search out and hook up to. When that happens, the miraculous begins to occur. The woman with the issue of blood in Luke 8:42-48, the centurion's servant in Matthew 8:5-13, and the Canaanite woman in Matthew 15:22-28 are examples of people activating their faith to obtain God's mercy and grace. Wherever you are, if you have faith, the glory of God can find you.

Chapter 5: *Power for Everyone*

WHY IS THE TOASTER NOT WORKING

My wife and I along with our neighbors enjoy a wonderful commodity that is available to us in our community. It is the public utility of electricity. Because of it, we have the ability and power to operate wonderful conveniences and run many things in our homes. This electrical power is generated by a power station and is transferred to communities by way of relay stations, transformers, and power lines. Our homes are wired to receive and make use of that electrical current. If for any reason the power is cut off or interrupted along the way, every home and every individual in the community suffers in darkness. And so it is in God's kingdom, when man has no power connection with God, the robe of glory (ability, holiness, power, wisdom, and righteousness) is cut off, leaving us vulnerable. People began to wonder why bad things happen and why things aren't working.

When there is no robe of power in the local church, what you have is a social club. When there is no robe of integrity in government, what you have is demagoguery. When there is no robe of righteousness in society, what you are left with is lawlessness. Unfortunately, the distressing part of this dilemma is when these things are allowed to linger among men, they become accepted as normal ways of living. After a while, the old landmarks and boundaries are removed so that righteous standards are mocked and sneered at.

Proverbs 22:28 NKJV

Do not remove the ancient landmark, which your fathers have set.

The eventual result is political, religious, and social nihilism. This way of living is so far below God's high life that He had planned for man.

What the religious community does not understand is that Jesus laid aside the glory He had with the Father in heaven and came to earth to live as a man. Jesus came not only to save but to demonstrate what a man who has maintained his connection with God and is still wrapped in a robe of glory should look and live like.

John 14:7-12 NKJV

"If you had known Me, you would have known My Father also; and from now on you know Him and have seen Him." Philip said to Him, "Lord, show us the Father, and it is sufficient for us." Jesus said to him, "Have I been with you so long, and yet you have not known Me, Philip? He who has seen Me has seen the Father; so how can you say, 'Show us the Father'? Do you not believe that I am in the Father, and the Father in Me? The words that I speak to you I do not speak on My own authority; but the Father who dwells in Me does the works. Believe Me that I am in the Father and the Father in Me, or else believe Me for the sake of the works themselves.

"Most assuredly, I say to you, he who believes in Me, the works that I do he will do also; and greater works than these he will do, because I go to My Father.

You see, in addition to faith in Jesus (the Word), God's glory is the answer for the church and the world. We need it, we must have it, and we can't live without it! In this day and time, the glory of God, which is the baptism of the Holy Ghost and fire, is the robe of righteousness and the outward expression of God's presence and authority in our lives. Bought by the blood of Jesus, this is a must-have for the church and for you and me. Otherwise, we struggle and then we just fall back into religious rituals. We go back to what is familiar and safe but expect a different outcome. Because we don't know what to do next, we cover ourselves with more temporary leaves to make it through.

It is very easy to use natural and religious solutions to fill the absence of the glory, but these things can never take the place of what man had lost, which was God's overflowing grace. The Bible is the account of God's plan to get His life and glory back to every man and woman. It's the "Good News."

This is power for everyone in the community, not to be cloistered behind walls and not for an elect group, but as many as receive.

John 1:10-14 NKJV

He was in the world, and the world was made through Him, and the world did not know Him. He came to His own, and His own did not receive Him. But as many as received Him, to them He gave the right to become children of God, to those who believe in His name: who were born, not of blood, nor of the will of the flesh, nor of the will of man, but of God. And the Word became flesh and dwelt among us, and we beheld His glory, the glory as of the only begotten of the Father, full of grace and truth.

Is There a Power Outage?

There is nothing more frustrating to a man or woman than to come home from work to a power outage. At that point, you are inconvenienced in every way possible. The electrical power that so easily flowed to you earlier is now cut off. You scramble to find another way to get things done. Doesn't that sound just like what God would do? God would cut off power to His church so that they can find another way to get things done, never! Some men claim that the day of the apostles and prophets has passed away. Whether you know it or not, the apostles, prophets, pastors, teachers, and evangelists are the distribution lines of the power of God to the church and to you. Yes, the original Twelve Apostles and the prophets of old have passed, but the office (position) and the anointing on those offices remain. It can be more easily explained in this manner. All the men who have held the office of the President of the United States could have passed away and the office may be vacant, but the position, power, honor, prestige, and respect due the President remains.

Ephesian 4:11-16 NKJV

And He Himself gave some to be apostles, some prophets, some evangelists, and some pastors and teachers, for the equipping of the saints for the work of ministry, for the edifying of the body of Christ, till we all come to the unity of the faith and of the knowledge of the Son of God, to a perfect man, to the measure of the stature of the fullness of Christ; that we should no longer be children, tossed to and fro and carried about with every wind of doctrine, by the trickery of men, in the cunning craftiness of deceitful plotting, but, speaking the truth in love, may grow up in all things into Him who is the head--Christ-- from whom

WHAT EVERY MAN NEEDS TO KNOW

the whole body, joined and knit together by what every joint supplies, according to the effective working by which every part does its share, causes growth of the body for the edifying of itself in love.

Some men may say that we don't need the apostles and prophet gifts anymore because we now have the Bible. The five gifts that Jesus gave us in Ephesians 4:11 are the Hand of God's government upon the church. Each one of these spiritual gifts has a different voice and a different spiritual talent and assignment that will help mature and perfect the church.

A few years ago, we had the privilege of visiting the Empire State Building. From the highest observation deck, you can see up to eighty miles. From that vantage point, you can see what weather conditions are coming your way. You can see every area that is congested with traffic and people and areas that are clear. You have insight on which way to go and which way not to go, because you have a different perspective than those on the ground. Those people on the ground are surprised by everything that comes upon them because they don't have your orientation. On the other hand, if they had communication from someone at your vantage point, they would have invaluable information.

In addition, if the person with such a high vantage also had the power to change situations at the ground level, they would be like a master chess piece that would not come off the board until the match was over. If there is a break in communication, there will be a shortage of available power. This is the description of only part of the ministry of the apostle and the prophet. If I were an enemy, I would do my best to convince my opponent that these two spiritual dynamos of church government are no longer necessary. Don't be fooled by the wiles of the Devil!

How Much More Power

Jesus was praying in a certain place, and when He finished, His disciples came and asked Him to teach them to pray also. John the Baptist had taught his disciples, but somewhere along their journey, they made the connection between Jesus's prayer life and the miracles they saw Him perform. So, like any good teacher, He gave them an example (a template) of prayer. You can call it an outline, which the person praying is expected to fill in with their personal worship and repentance to God. But what do we do? We religiously repeat the outline instead. We call this the Lord's Prayer.

Luke 11:2-4 NKJV

So He said to them, "When you pray, say: Our Father in heaven, Hallowed be Your name. Your kingdom come Your will be done On earth as it is in heaven. Give us day by day our daily bread. And forgive us our sins, For we also forgive everyone who is indebted to us. And do not lead us into temptation, But deliver us from the evil one."

The teaching continues as Jesus explains His Prayer. He uses an example of a friend showing up at an inopportune time. It was customary to refresh a guest with bread and wine after a journey and take care of any of their needs. Though you may be unprepared, you have a friend who always has more than enough bread, day or night. For ages, bread has been known as the staple of life and is used to strengthen and sustain a man. Jesus gave instructions to beat the door down with persistent asking, seeking, and knocking until you get what you need. You can only make this kind of annoying and shameless demand to a Covenant friend or a neighbor. He assures them that they will get what they need.

Luke 11:5-10 NKJV

And He said to them, "Which of you shall have a friend, and go to him at midnight and say to him, 'Friend, lend me three loaves; for a friend of mine has come to me on his journey, and I have nothing to set before him'; and he will answer from within and say, 'Do not trouble me; the door is now shut, and my children are with me in bed; I cannot rise and give to you'? I say to you, though he will not rise and give to him because he is his friend, yet because of his persistence he will rise and give him as many as he needs.

"So I say to you, ask, and it will be given to you; seek, and you will find; knock, and it will be opened to you. For everyone who asks receives, and he who seeks finds, and to him who knocks it will be opened.

Jesus assures them that they will get what they are praying for. They don't have to be concerned about being fooled or tricked because the friend with whom they are dealing with can be trusted.

Luke 11:11-12 NKJV

If a son asks for bread from any father among you, will he give him a stone? Or if he asks for a fish, will he give him a serpent instead of a fish? Or if he asks for an egg, will he offer him a scorpion?

Jesus concludes His teaching by telling His Disciples that the friend that they can go to at any time is their Heavenly Father and the Bread that they should be persistently seeking is not natural bread. It is not daily food or clothing nor any other physical item, as many supposed in Luke 11:3. It is the Bread of the Holy Ghost and fire. Finally, He reminds them of how much natural men love to spoil their children with good gifts. Then, how much more will their Heavenly Father spoil and lavish gifts upon His children who ask, seek, and knock with the Holy Ghost and fire. In short, His instruction to them was to pray until they overflow, then pray some more.

Luke 11:13 NKJV

If you then, being evil, know how to give good gifts to your children, how much more will your heavenly Father give the Holy Spirit to those who ask Him!"

How often do we come across a friend or co-worker, a family member, a church member, or a stranger that has cancer, a broken heart, an addiction, who has lost their way in life, or has a trouble of depression? Their help can be found in those who have gone to God and have been lavishly spoiled with His Glory. Jesus was manifested to destroy the works of the devil. How much more power do you need to meet the needs in your own family and in your community? It is available. Will you be wrapped in His Glory?

In our highly educated and industrialized western culture, our churches have sometimes relied on neat little liturgical packages for our services, instead of the Holy Spirit. They make us feel good and satisfy our conscience and religious itch, then we go home. In such instances, sadly and much too often, people who come with hidden needs leave empty-handed and unfulfilled. That is what is commonly known as man's religion. If the Holy Spirit of God is allowed to have freedom in those services, a great many problems in our communities would be solved.

It is the power, love, and compassion of the Holy Spirit that will change the lives of people inside and outside the church. Part of the problem is that the Christians in our western societies and cultures have little or no clue what power and authority has been given to them in Jesus Christ. As a result, we have relied on education and enlightenment as a substitute for the power and wisdom of God's Spirit. Many of our societal problems have a spiritual root cause, but because the average churchgoer's spiritual acumen is so low, their solutions sound just like the world's solutions.

Are you having problems in your family or church? Can you imagine one saint in your church covered with the robe of God's glory? I am not referring to the pastor, but someone who simply prays and gets results, someone who lays hands on the sick and they recover, someone who prays for the addict or bipolar and demonic yokes are broken from their necks, or someone who can pray and get God's wisdom and direction. Can you imagine if there were two such saints in your church? Imagine if there were three, four, five, or even a congregation full of such people. The power of God's presence would be exponentially multiplied each time they came together. They would be unstoppable in meeting the needs of the community. At the same time, they would cause praise and thanksgiving to abound to God for His goodness. That is God's plan for us.

If there are no such saints in your congregation, there should be. These are not special people who have been canonized, doctorized, or idolized. These are regular people who have given their hearts to Jesus and are baptized in the Holy Ghost and fire. When there is an absence of spirit-filled believers, there is a power disruption from God and there is always someone or something to fill the vacuum.

Because of his ministerial association, my pastor received a call from another pastor in Huntington, West Virginia. It seems that their church was having problems, but the source of those troubles was a mystery. So, their pastor asked if we could help them.

Sent by our pastor, Brother Gary and I arrived in Huntington on Saturday around 5:00 p.m. Not knowing what we were facing, we felt the need to spend that evening in prayer and fasting. Gary's wife, Colette, was scheduled to meet us on Sunday morning before church. Church service began with such powerful praise and worship that the atmosphere was palpable. It was so awesome and heavenly that I leaned over to Colette and said, "This is wonderful. Why do they need us?"

She replied, "I don't have a clue."

After a few songs, their pastor stepped forward and said, "After a selection from our Holy Ghost choir, the next voice you hear from the pulpit will be Reverend Gary." The room was still alive with God's tangible presence. After the pastor's announcement, an older woman got up and sat at the piano and their choir rose to sing. The moment she began to play, the wonderful presence created during praise and worship was completely gone. The thing that now filled the atmosphere in that room was not good; as a matter of fact, it felt dark and demonic. I was so shocked that I let out an audible gasp. I leaned close to Colette and asked, "What happened?"

She responded, "I don't know, but they're asking Gary to follow this; are you kidding me!"

Brother Gary stepped behind the lectern and for the longest and toughest fifteen minutes in history tried to minister to that congregation. It wasn't working, it was like plowing concrete, and if I must say so myself, "It wasn't pretty." If there's one thing I've learned about God, it is He will not be mocked or outdone. Whether you know it or not, God is very competitive. And He does not lose. If God is for you, who can be against you? If God is on your side, how can you be denied? Suddenly, Brother Gary slammed his Bible shut, looked them straight in the eye and challenged them with these words, "If you want prayer, come forward, if you need healing in your body come forward, or if you are having problems, come up here now!"

A tidal wave of people ran forward and flooded the altar. The sweet presence of the Holy Spirit that was there during praise and worship swept back in that sanctuary like a blast of cool summer breeze. The mass of people who were uninterested a minute earlier were now hungry and thirsty for a touch from God. Brother Gary was praying for people as quickly as he could, but the number of people continued to increase. Finally, he stopped and looked up and asked me to help him pray for people. Everything went well until I reached the older woman who played the piano and her friend. As I approached them, they began to shriek and scream. They were frozen with fear and shaking all over. They kept saying repeatedly, "Don't touch me and get away from me." I kept looking behind me to see who they were afraid of, but there was no one there but me. They were witches. Yes, you heard me right. They were witches. Every time that lady would play the piano, those dark spirits that she, her friend, and her granddaughter entertained daily would come inhabit (dwell and live in) her worship. What started as a tidal wave of people needing prayer soon swelled into a tsunami of bodies. Several people in the congregation left the building and went from door to door through the neighborhood inviting more people into the church service.

It was crazy. I had never seen anything like it before, but if you can believe it, it was about to go to another level. There was a loud bang at the back of the sanctuary as the double doors swung open wide, and in came a group of people pushing a hospital gurney. As Colette, Gary, and I approached the gurney, they snatched a blanket off revealing a young boy about eleven or twelve years old. We were shocked to see that he was in a full body cast. The only things that were showing were his head, his hands, and his feet. They told us that he had been run over by the school bus. You couldn't help but cry tears of compassion as we placed our hands on him and prayed. After a few moments of prayer, he began to wiggle and move his extremities and began to say emphatically that he was healed. Now, whether that happened at that moment or gradually, we don't know because of the body cast. I pray for him and thank God for his healing and wholeness every time he crosses my mind.

Who was clueless? The pastor was clueless as to what was happening in that church and community until we arrived that Sunday morning. The three of us were clueless about the extreme shifts in the spiritual atmosphere we experienced at the beginning of that service. I was clueless to why those women were shrieking and screaming, until Colette was privy to a conversation between the two ladies. Combined with Colette's insight from the Holy Spirit, we began to understand the situation that we had walked into. Usually, the average churchgoing Christian who is not clothed in God's Holy Ghost and fire typically remains clueless and is unaware of the authority and power afforded them by God through Jesus Christ. God has prepared a table for us in the presence of our enemies. There is great grace available in God's kingdom for you and power for everyone. My friend, it is not good to remain clueless.

Chapter 6: *Light the Fire Again*

EMBERS

Today, many people enjoy the modern convenience of a gas or electric powered fireplace, but there is just something wonderful and relaxing about a wood burning fire. The smells, the crackling, popping sounds, feeling of nostalgia, and cozy heat makes for a pleasant experience. When the flames die down and there seems to be no life left in the fire, there are still hidden embers alive just waiting to be stirred into a flame once again.

Since the fall of Adam and Eve in the garden, though hidden in plain sight, the Scriptures declare God's intention to redeem and restore man's glory. Throughout history, God has continually reached down and stirred up His hidden embers, the prophets, so that man would not lose hope in God's loving kindness. Time after time, God sent His prophets to kindle a flame in the waning hearts of mankind, until the fullness of His plan could be revealed.

Through the passage of time, man became almost entirely unaccustomed, unfamiliar, and sometimes uninterested in his former garment of God's glory. There was a man (hidden ember) sent from God, whose name was John. He came to point out and bear witness of the arrival of the light of the world (Jesus), and that through him all men might believe.

John 1:6-9 NKJV

There was a man sent from God, whose name was John. This man came for a witness, to bear witness of the Light, that all through him might believe. He was not that Light, but was sent to bear witness of that Light. That was the true Light which gives light to every man coming into the world.

John 1:19-23 NKJV

Now this is the testimony of John, when the Jews sent priests and Levites from Jerusalem to ask him, "Who are you?" He confessed, and did not deny, but confessed, "I am not the Christ." And they asked him, "What then? Are you Elijah?" He said, "I am not." "Are you the Prophet?" And he answered, "No." Then they said to him, "Who are you, that we may give an answer to those who sent us? What do you say about yourself?" He said: "I am 'The voice of one crying in the wilderness: "Make straight the way of the Lord," as the prophet Isaiah said."

Before John's birth, the Angel Gabriel was sent to Zacharias to announce his son's assignment on earth. This glory residing on John the Baptist, which was the spirit and power of Elijah, would once again cause the people to turn their hearts back to God in repentance and worship.

Luke 1:13-17 NKJV

But the angel said to him, "Do not be afraid, Zacharias, for your prayer is heard; and your wife Elizabeth will bear you a son, and you shall call his name John. And you will have joy and gladness, and many will rejoice at his birth. For he will be great in the sight of the Lord, and shall drink neither wine nor strong drink. He will also be filled with the Holy Spirit, even from his mother's womb. And he will turn many of the children of Israel to the Lord their God. He will also go before Him in the spirit and power of Elijah, 'to turn the hearts of the fathers to the children,' and the disobedient to the wisdom of the just, to make ready a people prepared for the Lord."

1 Kings 18:19-39 NKJV

Now therefore, send and gather all Israel to me on Mount Carmel, the four hundred and fifty prophets of Baal, and the four hundred prophets of Asherah, who eat at Jezebel's table." So Ahab sent for all the children of Israel, and gathered the prophets together on Mount Carmel. And Elijah came to all the people, and said, "How long will you falter between two opinions? If the LORD is God, follow Him; but if Baal, follow him." But the people answered him not a word.

Then Elijah said to the people, "I alone am left a prophet of the LORD; but Baal's prophets are four hundred and fifty men. Therefore let them give us two bulls; and let them choose one bull for themselves, cut it in pieces, and lay it on the wood, but put no fire under it; and I will prepare the other bull, and lay it on the wood, but put no fire under it. Then you call on the name of your gods, and I will call on the name of the LORD; and the God who answers by fire, He is God." So all the people answered and said, "It is well spoken."

Now Elijah said to the prophets of Baal, "Choose one bull for yourselves and prepare it first, for you are many; and call on the name of your god, but put no fire under it."

So they took the bull which was given them, and they prepared it, and called on the name of Baal from morning even till noon, saying, "O Baal, hear us!" But there was no voice; no one answered. Then they leaped about the altar which they had made.

And so it was, at noon, that Elijah mocked them and said, "Cry aloud, for he is a god; either he is meditating, or he is busy, or he is on a journey, or perhaps he is sleeping and must be awakened." So they cried aloud, and cut themselves, as was their custom, with knives and lances, until the blood gushed out on them. And when midday was past, they prophesied until the time of the offering of the evening sacrifice. But there was no voice; no one answered, no one paid attention.

Then Elijah said to all the people, "Come near to me." So all the people came near to him. And he repaired the altar of the LORD that was broken down. And Elijah took twelve stones, according to the number of the tribes of the sons of Jacob, to whom the word of the LORD had come, saying, "Israel shall be your name." Then with the stones he built an altar in the name of the LORD; and he made a trench around the altar large enough to hold two seahs of seed. And he put the wood in order, cut the bull in pieces, and laid it on the wood, and said, "Fill four waterpots with water, and pour it on the burnt sacrifice and on the wood." Then he said, "Do it a second time," and they did it a second time; and he said, "Do it a third time," and they did it a third time. So the water ran all around the altar; and he also filled the trench with water.

And it came to pass, at the time of the offering of the evening sacrifice, that Elijah the prophet came near and said, "LORD God of Abraham, Isaac, and Israel, let it be known this day that

You are God in Israel and I am Your servant, and that I have done all these things at Your word. Hear me, O LORD, hear me, that this people may know that You are the LORD God, and that You have turned their hearts back to You again."

Then the fire of the LORD fell and consumed the burnt sacrifice, and the wood and the stones and the dust, and it licked up the water that was in the trench. Now when all the people saw it, they fell on their faces; and they said, "The LORD, He is God! The LORD, He is God!"

Finally, they were a people ready to take part in God's plan of restoration. The appointed season to unveil God's plan had arrived and man was poised on the threshold of God's kingdom.

Then Jesus came from Galilee to the Jordan River to be baptize by John. As He rose from the baptismal waters of the Jordan, He was praying. The heavens opened and the Holy Spirit descended in bodily form like a dove. It did not say that the Holy Spirit was a dove. It declares that the Spirit was in the shape of a body garment and descended and lighted upon Him gently like a dove.

Luke 3:21-22 NKJV

When all the people were baptized, it came to pass that Jesus also was baptized; and while He prayed, the heaven was opened. And the Holy Spirit descended in bodily form like a dove upon Him, and a voice came from heaven which said, "You are My beloved Son; in You I am well pleased."

That statement just destroyed two thousand years of religious thinking and made every demon angry. Whether you believe this or not is irrelevant, because what God just did before our eyes was to restore the garment of glory and light to His last Adam (Jesus). God in His mercy did what no man could do. Ignoring the frailties and weakness of the flesh, God laid asideHhis glory and came to earth in a human body (Jesus). This Man, God's holy ember, possessed the DNA and life blood of His Father God, which He would use to ransom man from his fallen state and restore the flame of God's glory to all who received Him (John 1:11-14). What a gracious gift to all mankind. From this one new Adam, God planned to set the whole of men's hearts everywhere ablaze with His glory. To as many as would receive His sacrifice, He would light the fire once again.

God's Bonfire

If you have ever gone to a bonfire at night, you have experienced something special. The warmth and power of the blazes, the camaraderie and the excitement of the event makes everyone feel euphoric. The same atmosphere that is enjoyed from a cozy fire in the privacy of the home is multiplied exponentially at a bonfire. Like flames in a fireplace, a bonfire can be described as a controlled burn. It is God's intention that everyone in your family and community experiences the warmth and power of His glory.

There are occasions when Almighty God pours out His Holy Ghost and fire upon a group of people, a church, a community, or a nation who are hungry and thirsty for His presence. In such cases, those people experience not a bonfire, but a sweeping wildfire of God's amazing love and grace. That's exactly what occurred on the Day of Pentecost. The flames of God's loving kindness swept three thousand souls into the kingdom of God (Acts 2:1-41). In one fell swoop, God restored His robe of glory to the whole earth. God is faithful to keep His promises. He will fill the earth with His glory. Need I remind you of Pentecost, the Protestant Reformation, the Welsh revival, the first and second Great Awakenings, the 1857 prayer revival, Azusa Street, the Charismatic Renewal, Asbury, and the Pensacola revivals? I implore you, don't limit God's grace because this doesn't fit your religious doctrine.

Habakkuk 2:14 NKJV

For the earth will be filled with the knowledge of the glory of the Lord, As the waters cover the sea.

It Only Takes a Spark for a Wildfire

Norm and Brenda were friends of ours and members of the same local church. My wife and I attended a Bible study in their home twice a month. Unless they were out of town, they were faithful to come to church. They had an infectious joy about the things of God and helped in ministry any way they could. Their youngest child, Ken, did not share their same enthusiasm. Every Sunday morning, Norm and Brenda would drag his behind to church. Ken was about fifteen or sixteen years old. He was not interested in the youth ministry, the praise and worship, nor the sermons. All he ever did was sit in one of the back rows and sleep until it was time to go home.

Ken was the usual bored teenager. During his senior year, he and other friends began to make pipe bombs to blow up things. They created these devices just for their entertainment. On one occasion, while making a pipe bomb, one of them exploded in Ken's hands. It did not kill him, but it burned and scarred his hands, arm, chest, and parts of his face. Shrapnel was embedded all over his body and cuts were everywhere. There was concern about him losing sight in an eye, but our church family prayed, and things worked out fine.

Up to that point, Ken was not interested in church and less interested in school. His grades were not good, but with two grading periods left to better them, he worked hard to pull them up. He got admission to Oral Roberts University and thrived as a student. Right before our eyes, we watched the Lord kindle an eternal spark in a young man's heart, one who was totally bored with life. He would never be the same again.

During his senior year at Oral Roberts University, he was part of a missionary team that was sent to Africa to help with a group of evangelistic crusade meetings. The meetings were held at night under an open sky. There were tens of thousands of people who were hungry and thirsty for the presence of God's Holy Ghost and fire. The first night, a tremendous thunderstorm threatened to cancel the meeting. The people began to pray and the two men conducting the meeting, T.L. Osborn and Archbishop Benson Idahosa, stepped forward and waved their hands to the Nigerian sky. Ken was amazed. The clouds opened and the stars came out and the meetings were a great success.

At the conclusion of the mass meetings in Nigeria, smaller localized services were planned for the surrounding townships, which would be led by pastors on stage. Ken was quite surprised and terrified when he was told that he and each of the Oral Roberts students that came with him was considered a pastor in these local meetings. He was not a licensed minister, never led a Bible study, nor had he spoken in public, but by this time, Ken was baptized with the Holy Ghost and fire. The pastor of the local church told Ken that the people were excited to hear what he had to say. Ken was thinking to himself, "God help us!"

The meeting began and great excitement and expectation filled the atmosphere. The local pastor introduced Ken and the people roared in praise to God. Ken, in a reserved, unassuming, and nervous manner, told them that God loved them so much that He sent Jesus to restore their relationship with Him and whoever accepted that would be saved. As he finished speaking, he was still shaking like a leaf from nervousness, but was relieved that it was finally over, or so he thought. The people began to cheer and praise the Lord. The local pastor stepped forward and thanked Ken for a wonderful message, then the pastor turned to the people and said, "If you would like Pastor Ken to pray for you, please come now." Ken did not show it, but he was horrified and was thinking, "What if nothing happens, what am I going to do?" Have you ever been there? Lord, help us when we call!

A line of hungry souls pushed towards the front. The first person in line was a woman. The local pastor said, "Pastor Ken this woman has been blind since birth. She would like for you to pray that Jesus would heal her eyes so she can see."

"Really," Ken thought to himself, "why can't it be something simple like a common cold?" Utterly terrified, Ken placed his hands on her and closed his eyes because he couldn't bear to watch. He began to pray and suddenly, the woman began to shout, "I can see!" She shouted those words over and over.

The place exploded with joy and praise. No one was more surprised and relieved than Ken. Every heart was ablaze with God's glory. There were many other miracles that occurred that day. Just think, this outpouring of God's glory was connected to a spark of flame started in the heart of a teenager who was bored with life.

Ken told us this story as we were working on a ministry project together just a few months after returning from Nigeria. When he finished telling the story, he looked at us and said, "You never know what's inside you if you don't use it." A spark is a witness that there is a flame available, a flame is a witness that there is a fire available, and a fire is a witness that there is a wildfire available to anyone who dares to believe. Jesus didn't come and give His life to make us a Baptist, He didn't come and give His life to make us a Methodist, He didn't come and give His life to make us a Catholic, nor did He come and give His life to make us a Pentecostal. He came to make us witnesses of His existence and grace.

Chapter 7: *Catching Men*

THE HUMAN BILLBOARD

Matthew 5:14-16 NKJV

You are the light of the world. A city that is set on a hill cannot be hidden. Nor do they light a lamp and put it under a basket, but on a lampstand, and it gives light to all who are in the house. Let your light so shine before men, that they may see your good works and glorify your Father in heaven.

That sounds ridiculous, doesn't it? The writer declares that the proper place for this light is on a lamp stand, where it can give sight to everyone in the room from its glow. From the very beginning, God intended to display Jesus like a billboard of His glory and majesty for all to see. Everyone who crossed His path and everyone that heard Him speak knew He was different from all the other rabbinical teachers. He spoke with wisdom and authority. He freed them from demonic oppression and healed their sicknesses. He was a sign and wonder from God that they could not ignore. It was not uncommon for rabbis and teachers to have followers, but hundreds and thousands were something out of the ordinary.

Luke 5:1-11
(paraphrased)

And it came to pass, the people pressed in on him so much that he climbed into a nearby boat belonging to Peter. He sat down and taught the people from there, and when he had finished, he asked them to launch out to the deep water for a catch. Peter explained how they had toiled all night and caught nothing. But out of respect, they would honor his request. Peter and his partners were professional fisherman who were quite familiar with the Lake of Gennesaret, its conditions, and the fish in it.

What they were not familiar with was the glory of God. When they let down the nets for a catch, so many fish filled the nets they began to break. They were filling the boat and could not handle the tremendous load of fish. So, they beckoned their fishing partners to help. The load of fish began to sink their boats, but the same glory that was filling the nets was also keeping the boats afloat.

Who fishes in the broad daylight with a net where the fish can plainly see you? Who fishes at a time when fish are not feeding near the surface? Who fishes in a place where you randomly cast the nets and land a year's supply of fish? Similar questions must have run through their minds. Peter, John, and James were astonished by what they had witnessed. In the natural, this was an impossible task, but not for a man covered with God's gory. They got a glimpse of something wonderful, something glorious, and something holy. With sudden feelings of unworthiness and remorse in his heart, Peter fell to his knees in worship. But Jesus, in His mercy, calmed all their fears and said, "From now on, I will teach you to catch men," instead of fish.

When they arrived back on land, they left everything to Zebedee
(the father of John and James) and followed Jesus.

What an outlandish promise to a bunch of country fishermen. The light of the world was willing to give to a flock of unlearned nobodies the glory that Adam lost in the garden. They were not the scholars of the day, the rich and famous, nor the strong and powerful, but they were the hungry, the thirsty, and the humble. Once those men experienced the glory of God, they would never be the same. Their lives were changed forever. They too would become shining lights adding to the brightness of God's lamp stand (Jesus). Now that the unlimited and inexhaustible ability of man's future was on display, who could resist God's goodness, can you?

Make You a Witness

It is an instinctive sentiment of those who have given their hearts to Jesus to be a witness of God's saving grace. It is the love of God that compels a man to seek the lost, the broken, and the downtrodden. It is God's love that causes a man to repent. Too often in the church world, we try to win men's hearts with our persuasive arguments, or tell them they are going to hell, or by meeting their physical needs. Those are natural means, but usually have little or no effect on men's spiritual lives. Jesus told His disciples that He would make them fishers of men. Just how was He going to do that? He instructed them to remain in Jerusalem and not to depart until they were clothed from heaven with God's promised robe of glory.

Acts 1:1-8 NKJV

The former account I made, O Theophilus, of all that Jesus began both to do and teach, until the day in which He was taken up, after He through the Holy Spirit had given commandments to the apostles whom He had chosen, to whom He also presented Himself alive after His suffering by many infallible proofs, being seen by them during forty days and speaking of the things pertaining to the kingdom of God.

And being assembled together with them, He commanded them not to depart from Jerusalem, but to wait for the Promise of the Father, "which," He said, "you have heard from Me; for John truly baptized with water, but you shall be baptized with the Holy Spirit not many days from now." Therefore, when they had come together, they asked Him, saying, "Lord, will You at this time restore the kingdom to Israel?" And He said to them,

"It is not for you to know times or seasons which the Father has put in His own authority. But you shall receive power when the Holy Spirit has come upon you; and you shall be witnesses to Me in Jerusalem, and in all Judea and Samaria, and to the end of the earth."

It was important that they didn't try to accomplish their great commission without being fully clothed in the whole armor of God's presence. Have you been? It is this garment of God's love and power that captures men's hearts. We have this treasure in earthen vessels (fleshly bodies) that the excellency of the glory may not be of us, but of God. A spark needs no instructions to start a flame, a flame needs no teacher to start a fire, and a fire needs no director to start a blaze. That's the innate nature and potential of a single spark. A spark is a witness unto itself and so is the robe of God's glory on a believer. A man clothed from on high with the Holy Ghost doesn't have to go try to be a witness, because the witness lives in and flows out of him. He has chosen to put on God's cloak of glory whose nature is goodness and grace. That suit of glory can be viewed as the armor of God's goodness. If any man is touched by God's goodness, his heart will respond. So, let every believer put on the whole armor of God.

Destroy Every Vestige

John and Jason were father and son coworkers of mine, whose names I have changed to protect their privacy. Jason, the son, and I worked in the same department. Usually, I would ask how his family was doing. This particular day Jason told me that his mother had been diagnosed with cancer and the doctor's report was not good. Then, he asked if I would come to his parents home to pray for her. Of course, my answer was, "Yes." When I arrived at their home, his parents were seated at the dining room table. I was quite surprised to be greeted with such a joyous atmosphere of hope and expectation (faith), but this attitude came easy to them because these were church people, who still believed that Jesus paid a price for us to be healed today. Their faith was not corrupted by religious naysayers. So, I simply laid my hands on his mom and prayed for her to be healed in Jesus' name. As we prayed, we could feel the tangible presence of the Holy Spirit. There was nothing left to do but thank God for his goodness and wait for the next doctor's examination. You can imagine the joy and excitement we all had when the next report came back and there was no cancer in his mom's body.

My life was dramatically changed that day, not because of Jason's mom, but because of what followed our prayer in the dining room. The family led me to a bedroom at the back of their home. As I entered the room, I was shocked to see a giant cage-like structure that took up most of the floor space. Suddenly, a beautiful young woman stood up in the middle of that cage with a huge smile on her face. At that moment, I realized, it was not a cage but a large crib for an adult. My heart was broken. She was Jason's sister. As a toddler, she fell ill and had a prolonged temperature of 104 to 107 degrees for several days. She had severe brain damage. Now, she was thirty years old, but had the mind of a one and a half years old child. I burst into tears. I was stunned and speechless and did not pray for her at that time. I left their home with the intention of returning as soon as possible.

Lord, fill us with Your glory so that we might serve compassion to everyone in need. Give us courage and grace to meet every challenge. Help us to destroy every vestige of religion, every trace of doubt, and unbelief, so we don't block the flow of Your goodness. Your desire is for every man, woman, and child to be touched by Your glory, every home be blanketed with Your wisdom, and every nation be saturated with Your presence. Yes, Lord, Your glory is for me and my neighbor.

Using the Right Bait

For some time, I had worked as a lead designer in an engineering department of a major corporation. Many of my friends and coworkers are avid fishermen. In addition to their boats, they have a myriad of fishing tackle and gadgets. It is always interesting to hear them talk about the different lures and techniques they use to catch fish. Whether it is a jig, a spinner, or a crank bait, they seem to be relatively successful. At any given moment, the type of lure they used was critical to whether they were going to have a good day. More importantly, their knowledge of the effects of the seasons, the water conditions, temperatures, weather, and the tendencies of the fish were all factors to their ability to be able to catch the big one. Yes, it certainly seemed that my friends had armed themselves with enough wisdom to outsmart their prey. But God has a different mode of operation. He fishes for the hearts of men, not with lures of deception, but with a lure of His grace and glory.

You never know what's going on behind your neighbor's closed doors, with your coworker, with your fellow student, with the person sitting next to you on an airplane, or in church, unless they say something. Even if you were aware of their circumstances, would you be able to help in any way?

The Glory is for You and Your Neighbor

Dave was six feet seven inches tall and two hundred and sixty pounds. He was an Iron Man and Tuff Guy competitor. On the weekends, he would get in the ring and fight against forty- nine other men in a round robin tournament, no holds barred. The winner was the last man standing. He had worked as a bouncer at a local bar. One night, while working that job, he was knifed by a motorcycle gang in a brawl. This lifestyle had taken its toll on him and now he was experiencing problems with his back. There were days that he suffered in extreme agony from his back pain. Now, it was unbearable.

We were coworkers and became close friends. Occasionally, he would ask me questions about the Bible. To my surprise, he didn't show up for work one day and was absent for a few days. He returned about a week later to retrieve some medical insurance paperwork with the intention of leaving immediately afterwards. He informed me that he was having back surgery later that day and asked if I would pray with him before he left. We went to an empty office space where we would not disturb anyone else. Dave stood with his hands resting on the desk and I placed my hand on his back and began to pray. A wonderful sense of God's presence seemed to surround us. I could feel a warm tingling sensation in my hand. By this time, Dave was trembling with one hand holding the desk tightly and the other hand raised high in the air in reverence. We prayed for about three minutes, said goodbye, then before he left, he turned to me and said he would like to give his heart to Jesus. What a precious moment that was. This all occurred on a Friday.

The following Monday morning Dave showed up at work with a huge smile on his face. "What are you doing here?" I asked. He said he had checked into the hospital and prior to prepping him for surgery, they did more x-rays. While Dave and his wife were in a prep room, his surgeon came in scratching his head. He said he was puzzled and put up two sets of x-rays. The first set was from a week or so earlier. They displayed a spine with some missing discs and some additional damage. The surgeon simply described it as a hole in his back. Next, he put up the x-rays that were just taken. These x-rays showed a spine that was perfect, with no damage and no missing discs. Dave lay in the bed with one hand raised up in reverence to God. Meanwhile, Dave's wife, Connie, is repeatedly asking him, "What's going on?"

The surgeon said, "There's nothing wrong with you. Get dressed and go home."

During that weekend, Dave told Connie the whole story and she too decided to give her heart to Jesus. Connie's brother and his wife visited, heard what happened, they made the same decision. I think, by any measure, that would be called a great day of fishing. Glory to God for His wonderful mercy.

The most interesting part of Dave's testimony was his description of our three minutes of prayer in that office on Friday morning. He said when I placed my hand on his back, he didn't know how it was possible, but he could see fire flowing from my hand into his back. At that point, to keep from falling to the floor, he began to hold on to the desk tightly and was quite relieved when I removed my hand. He said that he sensed a change in his body but wasn't sure until he saw the xrays at the hospital.

You never know what circumstances people are facing until you pull back the curtains of their private sanctuaries. They may be highly successful people, but unfulfilled in their hearts. There may be hurt, or depression. There may be family incest or abuse. There may be addictions or abandonment. There may be a chronic illness or just plain fear. Sometimes only God knows, and He wants to use His people who are covered with His glory to make a difference in these lives and ultimately give them an answer to their question. If God is a good God, why are these things happening?

Chapter 8: *Selective Sensitivity Conditioning*

DULL OF HEART

It is amazing how something can be right in front of your eyes and you don't even notice it. An odor can be all around you and you can't smell it. A large train can be barreling down on you, blasting its horn repeatedly, and you don't hear it. Why? The answer is because of selective sensitivity conditioning. You can see, smell, and hear something so much that your senses become dull to those stimuli.

Matthew 13:10-17 NKJV

And the disciples came and said to Him, "Why do You speak to them in parables?" He answered and said to them, "Because it has been given to you to know the mysteries of the kingdom of heaven, but to them it has not been given. For whoever has, to him more will be given, and he will have abundance; but whoever does not have, even what he has will be taken away from him. Therefore I speak to them in parables, because seeing they do not see, and hearing they do not hear, nor do they understand. And in them the prophecy of Isaiah is fulfilled, which says: 'Hearing you will hear and shall not understand, And seeing you will see and not perceive; For the hearts of this people have grown dull. Their ears are hard of hearing, And their eyes they have closed, Lest they should see with their eyes and hear with their ears, Lest they should understand with their hearts and turn, So that I should heal them.'

"But blessed are your eyes for they see, and your ears for they hear; for assuredly, I say to you that many prophets and righteous men desired to see what you see, and did not see it, and to hear what you hear, and did not hear it.

A person may view something through only one colored lens, a pet owner may be nose-blind to his house pet odors, and a person living near the tracks could be conditioned to ignore train horn warning sounds. In certain of these cases, selective conditioning, such as alarm fatigue, can be dangerous and even fatal. Jesus referred to it as being dull of heart. A conditioned heart is a conformed or molded heart. Paul warns us not to see, hear, or think like the world, but be transformed into God's image by the renewing of our minds.

Romans 12:1-2 NKJV

I beseech you therefore, brethren, by the mercies of God, that you present your bodies a I beseech you therefore, brethren, by the mercies of God, that you present your bodies a living sacrifice, holy, acceptable to God, which is your reasonable service. And do not be conformed to this world, but be transformed by the renewing of your mind, that you may prove what is that good and acceptable and perfect will of God.

In the church, the problem we have with the Apostle Paul's mandate is not with the world, but with the interference of our selective religious conditioning. It is established and set up by man's denominations. From the very beginning, the Lord God Almighty intended for us to live in the glory mode. Just what does that mean or look like? It means He expects His children to act, think, and do the same things that He did. You may say that is an impossibility, because He is God, but I assure you that it is not. Jesus told His disciples that it was the Father in Him who does the work. Jesus completely relied on His Father's internal and overflowing glory to accomplish His mission, and we should do likewise. To a man who is lacking God's marvelous covering of glory, these things are an impossibility, but with God all things are possible to them who believe.

Because of our selective conditioning, many people miss the fourfold purpose of the ministry of John the Baptist and Jesus. At the appointed time, John the Baptist came on the scene to announce the advent of the season of the Christ. John went even further and pointed Him out to men.

John 1:29-36 NKJV

The next day John saw Jesus coming toward him, and said, "Behold! The Lamb of God who takes away the sin of the world! This is He of whom I said, 'After me comes a Man who is preferred before me, for He was before me.' I did not know Him; but that He should be revealed to Israel, therefore I came baptizing with water."

And John bore witness, saying, "I saw the Spirit descending from heaven like a dove, and He remained upon Him. I did not know Him, but He who sent me to baptize with water said to me, 'Upon whom you see the Spirit descending, and remaining on Him, this is He who baptizes with the Holy Spirit.' And I have seen and testified that this is the Son of God." Again, the next day, John stood with two of his disciples. And looking at Jesus as He walked, he said, "Behold the Lamb of God!"

Secondly, the Scriptures tell us that John's ministry was to turn the people's hearts in repentance to God and prepare them for their redemption (Luke 1:5-17). What we are most familiar with is the ministry of Jesus. He came to give His life as a ransom for man's sin. He shed His blood on the cross to redeem man once and for all from the power of his fallen state and Satan. At the same time, He restored man's broken relationship with God. What we have missed, what we have not understood, or seen is just as important as the three previous aspects mentioned above of the ministry of John the Baptist and Jesus. Jesus came to baptize us with the Holy Ghost and fire.

Luke 3:15-17 NKJV

Now as the people were in expectation, and all reasoned in their hearts about John, whether he was the Christ or not, John answered, saying to all, "I indeed baptize you with water; but One mightier than I is coming, whose sandal strap I am not worthy to loose. He will baptize you with the Holy Spirit and fire. His winnowing fan is in His hand, and He will thoroughly clean out His threshing floor, and gather the wheat into His barn; but the chaff He will burn with unquenchable fire.

Yes, He came to restore the garment of glory that Adam lost in the garden. The customary covering for a godly man is a cloak of God's light. Because of its importance, I must keep saying this to you. If it were not a vital, critical, crucial, integral, and necessary part of man's restoration, John would not have mentioned it at all. It is possible to receive the finished work of the cross and still live without God's covering of glory.

Acts 19:1-6 NKJV

And it happened, while Apollos was at Corinth, that Paul, having passed through the upper regions, came to Ephesus. And finding some disciples he said to them, "Did you receive the Holy Spirit when you believed?" So they said to him, "We have not so much as heard whether there is a Holy Spirit." And he said to them, "Into what then were you baptized?" So they said, "Into John's baptism." Then Paul said, "John indeed baptized with a baptism of repentance, saying to the people that they should believe on Him who would come after him, that is, on Christ Jesus." When they heard this, they were baptized in the name of the Lord Jesus. And when Paul had laid hands on them, the Holy Spirit came upon them, and they spoke with tongues and prophesied.

The problem with this spiritual state is the individual believer as well as the church would remain powerless to fulfill the Great Commission.

Matthew 28:18-20 NKJV

And Jesus came and spoke to them, saying, "All authority has been given to Me in heaven and on earth. Go therefore and make disciples of all the nations, baptizing them in the name of the Father and of the Son and of the Holy Spirit, teaching them to observe all things that I have commanded you; and lo, I am with you always, even to the end of the age." Amen.

John's testimony at the Jordan River was that Jesus Christ would baptize you with the Holy Ghost and fire. In short, He would make you look, act, think, and live like God the Father and His Son Jesus.

For the religious Pharisees out there, I did not say that you would be God nor His Son Jesus, but you would be restored to your rightful place in God's family. There is no way that we can continue to ignore all that the Lord has made available to those who call on His name. Everything that He has provided is right in front of our eyes and within our grasp that we might be successful. Do not let your human intellect or religious pride get in the way. There are people who need a touch of God's hand of grace through you.

Some Thirty, Some Sixty, Some One Hundred Fold

As a kid growing up, I spent most of my summers on my grandparents' farm. Every year, we planted a variety of crops all over those eighty-five acres of farmland. Even as a youngster, I learned very early in life that the harvest from the crops we planted was directly related to the condition of the soil and weather (temperature, sun, and moisture). Generally, we rely on nature to provide suitable weather conditions for a good harvest, but the condition of the soil is left entirely up to us. It is our responsibility to till the soil, fertilize it, dig out rocky places, and weed it. Most important of all, the seed that you plant must be a good seed, or you're wasting your time. The most fascinating thing about this whole process is the propagation and multiplication of all those seed plantings. Depending on the type of seedling, a single seed can produce hundreds or thousands of clones of itself. Those seeds that we planted in the ground had to die before they could live. The germination process is not a pretty thing. The warmth, moisture, and air combined with the chemical and mineral composition of the soil swells and breaks the seed cover and feeds that ugly little embryo. Not long afterwards, that seedling sprouts and grows to a mature plant that produces seeds of its own.

It is inherent for a seed to multiply once it has been planted. Have you ever wondered why some harvests are bountiful and some small. We often hear the phrase "some thirty, some sixty, or some a hundredfold" as it pertains to a return on our giving. According to the scriptures, your harvest in life depends entirely on the attitude of your heart and the kind of words (seeds) you allow to be planted there. If you allow words of truth to be planted, you get a harvest of truth and virtue, but if you allow lies to be planted, you get a harvest of lies and deception.

In the Parable of the Sower of seeds, Jesus describes the different types of soils (hearts) the seed (Word of God) is scattered upon. It is the unbelieving, the shallow, stony, and the thistle and thorn- riddled heart that never produces a mature harvest, because the condition of those soils allowed their circumstances to overpower the value and potential of the seed. What people have selectively trained their physical eyes and ears to receive can close their spiritual perception and shut them off from God's Glory.

Matthew 13:18-23 NKJV

Therefore hear the parable of the sower: When anyone hears the word of the kingdom, and does not understand it, then the wicked one comes and snatches away what was sown in his heart. This is he who received seed by the wayside. But he who received the seed on stony places, this is he who hears the word and immediately receives it with joy; yet he has no root in himself, but endures only for a while. For when tribulation or persecution arises because of the word, immediately he stumbles. Now he who received seed among the thorns is he who hears the word, and the cares of this world and the deceitfulness of riches choke the word, and he becomes unfruitful. But he who received seed on the good ground is he who hears the word and understands it, who indeed bears fruit and produces: some a hundredfold, some sixty, some thirty."

The seed (words and ideas) that you believe (plant) in your heart is just as important as the condition of the heart itself. Selective sensitivity conditioning can be a process (lens) through which a person chooses to filter their beliefs. God expects His children to filter their beliefs through His word of truth. When people filter their beliefs through their culture, their denomination, their politics, their race, their hurt, their anger, or bitterness rather than truth, they handcuff the Holy Spirit and diminish their harvest in life. How can there be a promise of as much as one hundred times, but get no return harvest at all? It is because God will only bless the truth in your heart and not man's feelings or opinions.

Phajaan

Almost everyone has seen or is familiar with the picture of a large elephant standing with a small rope or chain around his leg with a stake in the ground as an anchor to keep the elephant secure. In passing, you would think that massive beast could leave anytime he chooses, but he can't because of a process called phajaan. When that elephant was a baby, it was separated from its mother. The mother might have been acquainted with freedom and power in the wild and if left alone, she will teach her baby likewise. Phajaan is a process of crushing that baby elephant in a cage or box to break his will by restricting his movement. At times, they may place a heavy rope or chain around the animal's leg that is far too strong for him to break, but powerful enough to cause a very sore leg and conscience from his struggling. Though he is a very powerful beast, he has been psychologically conditioned by his circumstances and now he is easily controlled by a very small rope or chain and a stake in the ground.

This is not an unusual circumstance. It happens all the time; generally, we don't recognize it for what it is. After four hundred years, God got the Hebrews out of Egypt with great signs and wonders, but He couldn't get four hundred years of slavery in Egypt out of them. America, doesn't that sound familiar? That baby elephant can't pass down its psychological crushing, its bruises, its hurts, its degradation, its abuses, its humiliation, and its anger and bitterness, but men do that from generation to generation. Though a man may be physically free, the rope and chain can still be around his soul. He is easily triggered by every negative circumstance that conjures up memories of his ancestors' psychological crushing.

Flashing blue lights, a child that has been sexually abused, a wife that has been verbally or physically battered, a female that has been raped, a person with depression, someone who has been abandon, or a child with low self-esteem from an overbearing negative-speaking parent are all forms of phajaan. Just like that elephant, these kinds of psychological conditionings can keep an individual or an entire race of people constrained in their hearts. What's the answer? The answer is found at the cross of Calvary. That is where God intended for every man and people to dump and bury their baggage. He wants us to die to the past and be clothed with new life. God's heart breaks when people hurt, but He will not bless the pointing of fingers, the blame game, or the victim mentality. The power of the Holy Spirit, not religion, can destroy the yoke of phajaan and wrap you in God's loving kindness and glory.

Chapter 9: *The Glory Mode*

WHAT DOES THAT LOOK AND SOUND LIKE?

Since the Garden of Eden, all eternity has been waiting for this day. I can imagine that the entire heavenly family was standing and peering over the banisters of glory with great anticipation. The culmination of God's twofold restoration plan for man has finally been released into the earth. Almighty God and His son, the King of Glory, Jesus Christ, have cut a covenant with man in front of the whole world on Calvary. The exchange of His innocent life for our life of sin was complete. I am not calling you a sinner. In fact, you may be a very good person, who does many commendable things. I am referring to the sin nature handed down generation after generation through Adam and Eve's tainted blood line, which occurred when they ate from that poisonous tree in the garden. To pay the ransom for their disobedience, innocent, holy, pure, righteous, and undefiled blood must be shed in its place. This one act of obedience cleared the slate between God and man and restored their relationship.

Hebrews 2:14-18 NKJV

Inasmuch then as the children have partaken of flesh and blood, He Himself likewise shared in the same, that through death He might destroy him who had the power of death, that is, the devil, and release those who through fear of death were all their lifetime subject to bondage. For indeed He does not give aid to angels, but He does give aid to the seed of Abraham. Therefore, in all things He had to be made like His brethren, that He might be a merciful and faithful High Priest in things pertaining to God, to make propitiation for the sins of people. For in that He Himself has suffered, being tempted, He is able to aid those who are tempted.

Once and for all, Jesus paid man's debt and cleared man's conscience of sin and dead works.

Hebrews 10:10-14 NKJV

By that will we have been sanctified through the offering of the body of Jesus Christ once for all. And every priest stands ministering daily and offering repeatedly the same sacrifices, which can never take away sins. But this Man, after He had offered one sacrifice for sins forever, sat down at the right hand of God, from that time waiting till His enemies are made His footstool. For by one offering He has perfected forever those who are being sanctified.

On this much-awaited day, God fulfilled His twofold plan of man's restoration by flooding His disciples with the Holy Ghost and fire, therefore, making it possible for everyone to receive God's Robe of Glory once again.

Acts 1:4-8 NKJV

And being assembled together with them, He commanded them not to depart from Jerusalem, but to wait for the Promise of the Father, "which," He said, "you have heard from Me; for John truly baptized with water, but you shall be baptized with the Holy Spirit not many days from now." Therefore, when they had come together, they asked Him, saying, "Lord, will You at this time restore the kingdom to Israel?" And He said to them, "It is not for you to know times or seasons which the Father has put in His own authority. But you shall receive power when the Holy Spirit has come upon you; and you shall be witnesses to Me in Jerusalem, and in all Judea and Samaria, and to the end of the earth."

Acts 2:1-11
(Paraphrased)

When the season had fully come. There came a sound from heaven like a mighty rushing wind. A fresh blast of the breath of life was released into the earth from God. Then cloven tongues of fire appeared, which was God's breath and spoken glory manifested to them. It set on each of them and began flooding and defusing their souls.

They began to speak as the Spirit gave them utterance. They began to give audible expression to the sense of a wonderful divine presence that they felt.

They made a sound with their voices because of an endowment of anointing that was flooding their souls. They began to prophesy in other tongues. They declared the wonderful works of God and his tender mercies. They turned the world upside down.

God, who is so rich in mercy, literally brought us from a dead relationship with Himself to a new life of prominence in His family. Because of the operation of the Spirit of God, our old nature (man) was crucified and buried with Jesus Christ (our Lamb of substitution). Then, we were raised in glory a new man and seated in heavenly places with Jesus.

Galatians 2:20 NKJV

I have been crucified with Christ; it is no longer I who live, but Christ lives in me; and the life which I now live in the flesh I live by faith in the Son of God, who loved me and gave Himself for me.

We have been given the privilege of being joint heirs with Jesus Christ, which is a definite distinction undeserved by man. On the other hand, it is a wonderful display of God's tender mercies and loving kindness for all creation to see.

Ephesians 2:1-10 NKJV

And you He made alive, who were dead in trespasses and sins, in which you once walked according to the course of this world, according to the prince of the power of the air, the spirit who now works in the sons of disobedience, among whom also we all once conducted ourselves in the lusts of our flesh, fulfilling the desires of the flesh and of the mind, and were by nature children of wrath, just as the others.

But God, who is rich in mercy, because of His great love with which He loved us,even when we were dead in trespasses, made us alive together with Christ (by grace you have been saved), and raised us up together, and made us sit together in the heavenly places in Christ Jesus, that in the ages to come He might show the exceeding riches of His grace in His kindness toward us in Christ Jesus. For by grace you have been saved through faith, and that not of yourselves; it is the gift of God, not of works, lest anyone should boast. For we are His workmanship, created in Christ Jesus for good works, which God prepared beforehand that we should walk in them.

THE NEW GARDEN OF EDEN

From the moment that the disciples were baptized with the Holy Ghost and fire, they began to heal the sick, cleanse lepers, raise the dead, and cast out devils. They began to do what Jesus did, which was take dominion and subdue. Starting at Jerusalem, they began to cultivate their world with God's grace. From the day they were baptized with the Holy Ghost and fire, their deeds were chronicled in the Book of Acts. Can you say the same? If not, get baptized. It is the Holy Spirit Who wants to make you a witness of God's goodness in His garden, which is your family and community.

Show Me Your Glory

"Show me Your glory" is a request that Moses made to God that can be found in chapter thirty-three in the Book of Exodus. Moses was allowed to see God's back, but not His face. By this time, they had developed more than a God to man relationship. They had become friends, and when Moses asked to see His glory, God showed Moses His goodness. Every man would rather speak to his friend face to face. A man's face reveals the essence of who he really is inside. Every facial expression reveals what he's thinking, especially his eyes. What God is inside overflows and engulfs Him completely. To show Moses His eternal life from behind gave him a snapshot of God's essence, which is goodness and mercy to a friend. This is the same life that He breathed into Adam, the same life that flowed through and covered Jesus, and the very same life He offers you and me.

Exodus 33:12-23 NKJV

Then Moses said to the LORD, "See, You say to me, 'Bring up this people.' But You have not let me know whom You will send with me. Yet You have said, 'I know you by name, and you have also found grace in My sight.' Now therefore, I pray, if I have found grace in Your sight, show me now Your way, that I may know You and that I may find grace in Your sight. And consider that this nation is Your people."

And He said, "My Presence will go with you, and I will give you rest."

Then he said to Him, "If Your Presence does not go with us, do not bring us up from here. For how then will it be known that Your people and I have found grace in Your sight, except You go with us? So we shall be separate, Your people and I, from all the people who are upon the face of the earth."

So the LORD said to Moses, "I will also do this thing that you have spoken; for you have found grace in My sight, and I know you by name." And he said, "Please, show me Your glory."

Then He said, "I will make all My goodness pass before you, and I will proclaim the name of the LORD before you. I will be gracious to whom I will be gracious, and I will have compassion on whom I will have compassion." But He said, "You cannot see My face; for no man shall see Me, and live." And the LORD said, "Here is a place by Me, and you shall stand on the rock. So it shall be, while My glory passes by, that I will put you in the cleft of the rock, and will cover you with My hand while I pass by. Then I will take away My hand, and you shall see My back; but My face shall not be seen."

In the previous passage of scripture, Moses realized the importance of the presence of having God go along with them and he refused to move another step without Him. God's presence was their peace and security. The Lord has promised us the same through the blood of the Lamb and the power of the Holy Spirit.

Secondly, Moses realizes that the power of God's presence made them completely different than any other people on the face of the earth, and it was just as important to them that the rest of humanity was also aware of their uniqueness. God took them from among men and covered them with His presence for the express purpose of reaching you with His Grace.

1 Peter 2:9-10 NKJV

But you are a chosen generation, a royal priesthood, a holy nation, His own special people, that you may proclaim the praises of Him who called you out of darkness into His marvelous light; who once were not a people but are now the people of God, who had not obtained mercy but now have obtained mercy.

Chapter 10: *Coat of Many Colors*

REMEMBER THE PRISM?

When I was a kid in school, my science teacher decided to impress us by bringing a group of prisms to class to teach us about light. An optical prism is a transparent optical element with flat polished surfaces and angles designed to refract (bend and separate) white light into its many colors. It was amazing to see that white light was invisible to the naked eye, but the individual hues could be seen if they were reflected by different surfaces.

Likewise, the glory of God could not be observed on Jesus with the naked eye, except during His transfiguration, but was reflected when He spoke or touched things. The scriptures tell us that God is light, and just like natural light, God's glory has many different hues. His glory reflects the fruit of the Spirit mentioned in Galatians 5:22. In addition to these, His glory reflects grace, forgiveness, holiness, mercy, wisdom, and power. When these attributes are exercised, healing and deliverance occurs. A man who is clothed in God's invisible robe of many colors is fitted like Jesus with God's goodness. A man who is clothed in the robe of many colors has put on the whole armor of God and is fitted for the challenges brought by the prism of life. A man who is clothed in this manner has once and for all put off the rags of religion and put on God's truth and grace.

PUTTING ON YOUR WORK CLOTHES

A chef puts on an apron when he cooks, a painter puts on a smock when he creates, a policeman wears a uniform for authority, a doctor wears scrubs when he heals, and a soldier wears battle gear when he goes to war. If any of these members of society were not dressed properly, we would deem them somewhat ill prepared for their assignments. Likewise, if a man is not clothed in a garment of God's glory, he is inadequately prepared for life's challenges. I know that is a hard pill to swallow, and unfortunately, it is the norm in society. In no way, form or fashion is that God's will for you. It is the glory that saves, it is the glory that delivers, it is the glory that heals, it is the glory that brings peace and comfort, it is the glory that forgives, it is the glory that mends relationships, it is the glory that destroys strongholds, it is the glory that brings favor, it is the glory that brings joy, it is the glory that makes dreams come true, and it is the glory that does the work in a man's life.

2 Corinthians 4:1-7 NKJV

Therefore, since we have this ministry, as we have received mercy, we do not lose heart. - But we have renounced the hidden things of shame, not walking in craftiness nor handling the word of God deceitfully, but by manifestation of the truth commending ourselves to every man's conscience in the sight of God. - But even if our gospel is veiled, it is veiled to those who are perishing, whose minds the god of this age has blinded, who do not believe, lest the light of the gospel of the glory of Christ, who is the image of God, should shine on them. [5]For we do not preach ourselves, but Christ Jesus the Lord, and ourselves your bondservants for Jesus' sake. For it is the God who commanded light to shine out of darkness, who has shone in our hearts to give the light of the knowledge of the glory of God in the face of Jesus Christ. But we have this treasure in earthen vessels, that the excellence of the power may be of God and not of us.

What We Wear Makes a Difference

In the book of Genesis chapter thirty-seven, we are introduced to the youngest son of Jacob whose name is Joseph. Joseph was a prophetic dreamer and the favorite son of his father. To signify this, Jacob gives him a coat of many colors. His ten older brothers are extremely jealous of Joseph's favorite status and conceive a plan to get rid of him, even if it means murder. The brothers throw him in a pit and eventually sell him to a traveling caravan, but not before they strip Joseph of his coat of many colors and stain it with blood. To conceal their wicked deed, the brothers lie about Joseph's death and present the bloodied coat to their father as proof (Genesis 37:1-35).

The story of Joseph is an allegory of the life of Jesus and His multifaceted cloak of the Holy Ghost and fire, which was also given to Him by His Father. Like Joseph, the lovely, innocent, holy, and righteous garment of Jesus was also stained at the cross by His brethren (the Pharisees). Though the coat of many colors that Jesus wore was invisible to the natural eyes, the obvious results were miraculous. We do get a glimpse of His coat of glory on the Mount of Transfiguration.

Matthew 17:1-8 NKJV

Now after six days Jesus took Peter, James, and John his brother, led them up on a high mountain by themselves; and He was transfigured before them. His face shone like the sun, and His clothes became as white as the light. And behold, Moses and Elijah appeared to them, talking with Him. Then Peter answered and said to Jesus, "Lord, it is good for us to be here; if You wish, let us make here three tabernacles: one for You, one for Moses, and one for Elijah." While he was still speaking, behold, a bright cloud overshadowed them; and suddenly a voice came out of the cloud, saying, "This is My beloved Son, in whom I am well pleased. Hear Him!" And when the disciples heard it, they fell on their faces and were greatly afraid. But Jesus came and touched them and said, "Arise, and do not be afraid." When they had lifted up their eyes, they saw no one but Jesus only.

The coat of many colors was the source of great envy for the brothers of Joseph and the Pharisees of Jesus' day. To them, it was not only a statement of their father's blessing and favor, but also was indicative of Jesus and Joseph's impending rulership and birthright over their brethren.

Genesis 37:1-11 NKJV

Now Jacob dwelt in the land where his father was a stranger, in the land of Canaan. This is the history of Jacob. Joseph, being seventeen years old, was feeding the flock with his brothers. And the lad was with the sons of Bilhah and the sons of Zilpah, his father's wives; and Joseph brought a bad report of them to his father.

Now Israel loved Joseph more than all his children, because he was the son of his old age. Also he made him a tunic of many colors. - But when his brothers saw that their father loved him more than all his brothers, they hated him and could not speak peaceably to him.

Now Joseph had a dream, and he told it to his brothers; and they hated him even more. So he said to them, "Please hear this dream which I have dreamed: There we were, binding sheaves in the field. Then behold, my sheaf arose and also stood upright;

*and indeed your sheaves stood all around and bowed down
to my sheaf." And his brothers said to him, "Shall you indeed
reign over us? Or shall you indeed have dominion over us?" So
they hated him even more for his dreams and for his words.*

*Then he dreamed still another dream and told it to his brothers,
and said, "Look, I have dreamed another dream. And this time,
the sun, the moon, and the eleven stars bowed down to me." So he
told it to his father and his brothers; and his father rebuked him
and said to him, "What is this dream that you have dreamed?
Shall your mother and I and your brothers indeed come to bow
down to the earth before you?" And his brothers envied him,
but his father kept the matter in mind.*

John 11:45-52 NKJV

*Then many of the Jews who had come to Mary, and had seen
the things Jesus did, believed in Him. But some of them went
away to the Pharisees and told them the things Jesus did. Then
the chief priests and the Pharisees gathered a council and said,
"What shall we do? For this Man works many signs. If we let
Him alone like this, everyone will believe in Him, and the
Romans will come and take away both our place and nation."*

*And one of them, Caiaphas, being high priest that year, said
to them, "You know nothing at all, nor do you consider that
it is expedient for us that one man should die for the people,
and not that the whole nation should perish." Now this he did
not say on his own authority; but being high priest that year
he prophesied that Jesus would die for the nation, and not
for that nation only, but also that He would gather together
in one the children of God who were scattered abroad.*

The priestly garments worn by the Levites in the Old Testament were made of linen. This was a requirement while ministering in the temple because it symbolized an absence of human effort or exertion which would cause perspiration.

Ezekiel 44:17-19 MSG

"When they enter the gate complex of the inside courtyard, they are to dress in linen. No woolens are to be worn while serving at the gate complex of the inside courtyard or inside the Temple itself. They're to wear linen turbans on their heads and linen underclothes—nothing that makes them sweat. When they go out into the outside courtyard where the people gather, they must first change out of the clothes they have been serving in, leaving them in the sacred rooms where they change to their everyday clothes, so that they don't trivialize their holy work by the way they dress.

In those days, the priestly garments were to be worn only in sacred places. Now, the priestly garment of God's presence is to be worn on the sacred place of the human heart and was no longer confined to the temple grounds. Through the sacrifice of Jesus, we are invited to enter God's rest which the robe of God's glory provides. When compared to the spiritual, our natural abilities are limited and sometimes burdensome.

Matthew 11:28-30 MSG

"Are you tired? Worn out? Burned out on religion? Come to me. Get away with me and you'll recover your life. I'll show you how to take a real rest. Walk with me and work with me— watch how I do it. Learn the unforced rhythms of grace. I won't lay anything heavy or ill-fitting on you. Keep company with me and you'll learn to live freely and lightly."

So, you see, to be properly clothed, we are instructed by the scriptures to be filled with the Holy Ghost and fire, which is God's rest. My friend, I encourage you not to remain ill fitted for your "walk through life." Instead, seek to enter God's rest with all your heart today.

Hebrews 4:1-11 NKJV

Therefore, since a promise remains of entering His rest, let us fear lest any of you seem to have come short of it. For indeed the gospel was preached to us as well as to them; but the word which they heard did not profit them, not being mixed with faith in those who heard it. For we who have believed do enter that rest, as He has said: "So I swore in My wrath, 'They shall not enter My rest,'" although the works were finished from the foundation of the world. For He has spoken in a certain place of the seventh day in this way: "And God rested on the seventh day from all His works"; and again in this place: "They shall not enter My rest."

Since therefore it remains that some must enter it, and those to whom it was first preached did not enter because of disobedience, again He designates a certain day, saying in David, "Today," after such a long time, as it has been said: "Today, if you will hear His voice, Do not harden your hearts." For if Joshua had given them rest, then He would not afterward have spoken of another day. There remains therefore a rest for the people of God. For he who has entered His rest has himself also ceased from his works as God did from His. Let us therefore be diligent to enter that rest, lest anyone fall according to the same example of disobedience.

Many good Christian people have been born again and have a new spirit within them. They display many of the attributes of the fruit of the Spirit found in Galatians 5:22 (love, joy, peace, patience, kindness, goodness, faithfulness, gentleness, and self-control), but they have not been filled with the Holy Spirit and fire. The difference between the two lifestyles can be compared to driving a Yugo or driving a Ferrari; both get you to your same destination. Need I say more? A person who refuses to be filled with God's Holy Spirit and fire is left to a "works based" existence.

Chapter 11: *Your Sunday Best*

SHARK SKIN

Every adult remembers an outfit that their parents set aside for them to wear on special occasions or church. My mom bought me a sharkskin suit. I really don't know what color it was because every time the light hit that suit it changed from brown, to gray, to blue, to green. It all depended on how I moved in the light. When the sun reflected off that suit, I looked like ten kids in a neon light show. That was the nature of that fabric. You couldn't help but notice a person wearing a garment made of that material. Thank God! I quickly outgrew that suit before I was permanently scarred for life. When a man or woman is adorned in the garments of salvation and truth (God's robe of righteousness), they may be the most unassuming person in the world, but they are a dynamo in God's kingdom. They bring much glory to God's N.I.L (name, image, and likeness) in the heavens and on the earth.

Ol' Timey Church

In days gone by, people would reserve their best clothes for church, weddings, and formal occasions. Out of respect and reverence for God or the occasion, women wore their best dress and a beautiful hat on their head. Likewise, men would wear their best suit of clothing and a tie. The idea here is that people displayed reverence for sacred spaces. It is not good when people get so familiar with sacred places that they lose reverential etiquette in their dress, speech, or manners. Jesus gives us an example in the parable of the wedding feast.

Matthew 22:8-14 NKJV

"Then he said to his servants, 'The wedding is ready, but those who were invited were not worthy. Therefore go into the highways, and as many as you find, invite to the wedding.' So those servants went out into the highways and gathered together all whom they found, both bad and good. And the wedding hall was filled with guests. But when the king came in to see the guests, he saw a man there who did not have on a wedding garment. So he said to him, 'Friend, how did you come in here without a wedding garment?' And he was speechless. Then the king said to the servants, 'Bind him hand and foot, take him away, and cast him into outer darkness; there will be weeping and gnashing of teeth.' For many are called, but few are chosen."

THE NEW FIG LEAVES

During the 18th century, the Age of Enlightenment brought many intellectual ideas to the forefront. It promoted the ideas of individual liberties, religious tolerance, the scientific method, and individual reasoning. Combined with the creativity of the industrial revolution, this era of history lifted man to new heights. Since that time, man's knowledge has rapidly increased. New technological advances spring up almost daily. Because of these, some men believe that we have advanced to the place where God and His gifts are no longer needed. Many people have been quite successful through hard work and by using their natural abilities, giftings, and talents to attain lofty degrees, social notoriety, wealth, and power, which in the natural world are commendable accomplishments. Despite the wonderful efforts of man, no natural exertion can ever replace the overflowing glory lost in the Garden. When a man settles for these substitutes, it can only be described as modern-day fig leaves, especially in an era where a man's image and brand are held in high esteem across the social media platforms. This is a spiritual matter that can only be solved by faith in the death, burial, and resurrection of Jesus Christ.

Cleaned Up and Dressed Up

Under normal circumstances, it is not a good thing to be clothed in your best attire for any occasion without first bathing or washing your body. If some cleaning is not done, it is going to be an unpleasant experience for everyone around you. In cleaning, there is a display of proper respect for social and physical etiquette, which is a moral obligation and duty. The ol' folks used to say, "Cleanliness is next to godliness." Though this phrase can't be found anywhere in the scriptures, the concept is clearly expressed in the ritual washings of the Old Testament and by the cleansing power of the word and Holy Spirit in the New Testament. Washing is used figuratively for the believer's spiritual cleansing through the Word of God.

Ephesians 5:25-27 NKJV

Husbands, love your wives, just as Christ also loved the church and gave Himself for her, that He might sanctify and cleanse her with the washing of water by the word, that He might present her to Himself a glorious church, not having spot or wrinkle or any such thing, but that she should be holy and without blemish.

The Apostle Paul described salvation in Jesus Christ and the new birth by the power of the Holy Spirit as a spiritual washing: "He saved us by His grace."

Titus 3:5 NKJV

he saved us, not because of works done by us in righteousness, but according to his own mercy, by the washing of regeneration and renewal of the Holy Spirit

In the church world, for the last fifty years or so, the Holy Spirit has emphasized faith in the Word of God. During this time, He has stressed the importance of believing and receiving God's promises and truths found in the scriptures. Sure, there have been abuses by men and plenty of accompanying criticism, but as He promised, God's intent is to have an avenue to write His law of grace on a man's heart, and faith is that avenue. For without faith, it is impossible to please God.

Jeremiah 31:31-34 NKJV

"Behold, the days are coming, says the LORD, when I will make a new covenant with the house of Israel and with the house of Judah— not according to the covenant that I made with their fathers in the day that I took them by the hand to lead them out of the land of Egypt, My covenant which they broke, though I was a husband to them, says the LORD. But this is the covenant that I will make with the house of Israel after those days, says the LORD: I will put My law in their minds, and write it on their hearts; and I will be their God, and they shall be My people. No more shall every man teach his neighbor, and every man his brother, saying, 'Know the LORD,' for they all shall know Me, from the least of them to the greatest of them, says the LORD. For I will forgive their iniquity, and their sin I will remember no more."

Despite man's best efforts, no one can make himself clean and holy. It is done by the blood of Jesus, the washing of the water of the Word, and the sanctifying work of the Holy Spirit. As a result, faith in God's promises causes that Word to settle in a man's heart and produce a harvest of godly living and thinking. The scriptures describe it as a man who looks into the mirror of God's Word and is subsequently changed from one glory to another level of glory. In doing so, the "Word" Himself is washing and cleansing the blemishes of sin from the mind and heart while we look in the face of Jesus Christ.

2 Corinthians 3:17-18 NKJV

Now the Lord is the Spirit; and where the Spirit of the Lord is, there is liberty. But we all, with unveiled face, beholding as in a mirror the glory of the Lord, are being transformed into the same image from glory to glory, just as by the Spirit of the Lord.

What we wear and what we say emanates from the heart. Holiness begins there. Simply believing what God has said sets you apart from the rest of men on the earth. The entrance of God's Word into a man's life gives him light to live by and spiritual access to fellowship with God. Jesus declared that He delivered the Father's words of truth to the disciples, and because they believed what He told them, they were clean, sanctified, and set apart for God's suit of glory (the Holy Spirit).

John 17:6-22 NKJV

"I have manifested Your name to the men whom You have given Me out of the world. They were Yours, You gave them to Me, and they have kept Your word. Now they have known that all things which You have given Me are from You. For I have given to them the words which You have given Me; and they have received them, and have known surely that I came forth from You; and they have believed that You sent Me. "I pray for them. I do not pray for the world but for those whom

You have given Me, for they are Yours. And all Mine are Yours, and Yours are Mine, and I am glorified in them. Now I am no longer in the world, but these are in the world, and I come to You. Holy Father, keep through Your name those whom You have given Me, that they may be one as We are. While I was with them in the world, I kept them in Your name. Those whom You gave Me I have kept; and none of them is lost except the son of perdition, that the Scripture might be fulfilled.

But now I come to You, and these things I speak in the world, that they may have My joy fulfilled in themselves. I have given them Your word; and the world has hated them because they are not of the world, just as I am not of the world. I do not pray that You should take them out of the world, but that You should keep them from the evil one. They are not of the world, just as I am not of the world. Sanctify them by Your truth. Your word is truth. As You sent Me into the world, I also have sent them into the world. And for their sakes I sanctify Myself, that they also may be sanctified by the truth.

"I do not pray for these alone, but also for those who will believe in Me through their word; that they all may be one, as You, Father, are in Me, and I in You; that they also may be one in Us, that the world may believe that You sent Me. And the glory which You gave Me I have given them, that they may be one just as We are one."

It is the heart of a man that causes him to be fitted for glory. The grateful, the hungry, the meek, the humble, the pliable, and teachable hearts are the dwelling places of the Holy Spirit. The attitude of the heart will determine the altitude of your natural and spiritual life. There are many rich, powerful, and famous people who are spiritually bankrupt, and many poor people of low degree who are rich in spiritual attitude. Men will look on the outward appearance, but God looks at the heart. An extremely attractive woman who has a low self-esteem, a very handsome man who is arrogant, conceited, and chauvinistic, or a genius creator or inventor who has no people skills and is a donkey's rear end to work for are examples of cloaked character that God can easily see and weigh out. On the other hand, God will seek after and lavishly pour out His Holy Spirit on a man full of godly character.

1 Samuel 16:1-13 NKJV

Now the LORD said to Samuel, "How long will you mourn for Saul, seeing I have rejected him from reigning over Israel? Fill your horn with oil, and go; I am sending you to Jesse the Bethlehemite. For I have provided Myself a king among his sons."

And Samuel said, "How can I go? If Saul hears it, he will kill me."

But the LORD said, "Take a heifer with you, and say, 'I have come to sacrifice to the LORD.' Then invite Jesse to the sacrifice, and I will show you what you shall do; you shall anoint for Me the one I name to you."

So Samuel did what the LORD said, and went to Bethlehem. And the elders of the town trembled at his coming, and said, "Do you come peaceably?"

And he said, "Peaceably; I have come to sacrifice to the LORD. Sanctify yourselves, and come with me to the sacrifice." Then he consecrated Jesse and his sons, and invited them to the sacrifice.

So it was, when they came, that he looked at Eliab and said, "Surely the LORD's anointed is before Him!"

But the LORD said to Samuel, "Do not look at his appearance or at his physical stature, because I have refused him. For the LORD does not see as man sees; for man looks at the outward appearance, but the LORD looks at the heart."

So Jesse called Abinadab, and made him pass before Samuel. And he said, "Neither has the LORD chosen this one." Then Jesse made Shammah pass by. And he said, "Neither has the LORD chosen this one." Thus Jesse made seven of his sons pass before Samuel. And Samuel said to Jesse, "The LORD has not chosen these." And Samuel said to Jesse, "Are all the young men here?" Then he said, "There remains yet the youngest, and there he is, keeping the sheep."

And Samuel said to Jesse, "Send and bring him. For we will not sit down till he comes here." So he sent and brought him in. Now he was ruddy, with bright eyes, and good-looking. And the LORD said, "Arise, anoint him; for this is the one!" Then Samuel took the horn of oil and anointed him in the midst of his brothers; and the Spirit of the LORD came upon David from that day forward.

After reading the biblical account of David, it is plain to see that his heart and character were shaped and molded while shepherding his family's sheep out on the Judean hillsides. It was not a particularly glorious job. On the contrary, it was a dirty, smelly job and was at times quite boring. At other times, the work was labor intensive and dangerous. Walking the sheep back and forth to grazing land, to resting pastures, and to drinking water took effort. Caring for the wounds, bruises, and overall health of the flock was a constant duty. Keeping up with his flock numbers was important, and if any were missing, he would search and find the lost sheep. When it was necessary, he was willing to risk his life to rescue his flock from predators. In addition to caring for his family's sheep, it was this time of shepherding which David spent worshiping God and perfecting his musical skills.

The scriptures do not give us any record of David's older brothers tending the family's herd, but I am quite sure they did in their turn. In 1 Samuel 17:28 we get a glimpse of the older brothers' attitudes towards tending those sheep. They looked upon the job as menial and may have even despised those animals, while David invested his whole heart and life in the work of caring for them. That flock of sheep was valuable to the wellbeing of Jesse's family. It was the family's source of clothing, food, finances, and most important of all, those sheep were the family's lifeline of sacrifices and worship to God. Who knows, David may have imagined himself as a shepherd king out on those Judean hillsides and those sheep were his subjects.

My friend, you may be in a place where you think that God has forgotten you. You may be performing a task or job that seems unimportant and boring. You may be in a place where everyone has overlooked you, but God never forgets; He sees hard work and faithfulness, and He will not allow you to be overlooked. Right now, He is molding, and shaping, and fitting you for His glory.

Chapter 12: *Conclusion*

Jesus was sent into this world that every man and woman might have an abundant life. That does not necessarily mean a life full of things, but a life full of wholeness. A life filled with the overflowing presence of the Holy Spirit and a life that has access to God's loving kindness, that's God's plan for us. The outpouring and baptism of the Holy Ghost and fire is a guarantee of God's restoration for man.

In Luke chapter four, as was His usual custom, Jesus entered the synagogue in Nazareth and stood up to read from the Book of Isaiah. He read the proclamation of the season of God's restoration and declared the start of His public ministry.

Isaiah 61:1-11 NKJV

"The Spirit of the Lord GOD is upon Me,
Because the LORD has anointed Me
To preach good tidings to the poor;
He has sent Me to heal the brokenhearted,
To proclaim liberty to the captives,
And the opening of the prison to those who are bound;
To proclaim the acceptable year of the LORD,
And the day of vengeance of our God;
To comfort all who mourn,
To console those who mourn in Zion,

To give them beauty for ashes,
The oil of joy for mourning,
The garment of praise for the spirit of heaviness;
That they may be called trees of righteousness,
The planting of the LORD, that He may be glorified."
And they shall rebuild the old ruins,
They shall raise up the former desolations,
And they shall repair the ruined cities,
The desolations of many generations.
Strangers shall stand and feed your flocks,
And the sons of the foreigner
Shall be your plowmen and your vinedressers.
But you shall be named the priests of the LORD,
They shall call you the servants of our God.
You shall eat the riches of the Gentiles,
And in their glory you shall boast.
Instead of your shame you shall have double honor,
And instead of confusion they shall rejoice in their portion.
Therefore in their land they shall possess double;
Everlasting joy shall be theirs.
 "For I, the LORD, love justice;
I hate robbery for burnt offering;
I will direct their work in truth,
And will make with them an everlasting covenant.
Their descendants shall be known among the Gentiles,
And their offspring among the people.
All who see them shall acknowledge them,
That they are the posterity whom the LORD has blessed."
I will greatly rejoice in the LORD,

My soul shall be joyful in my God;
For He has clothed me with the garments of salvation,
He has covered me with the robe of righteousness,
As a bridegroom decks himself with ornaments,
And as a bride adorns herself with her jewels.
For as the earth brings forth its bud,
As the garden causes the things that are sown in it to spring
forth,
So the Lord GOD will cause righteousness and praise to spring
forth before all the nations.

What Does Every Man Need to Know?

This announcement was to proclaim the acceptable year of the Lord. It is the advent season of jubilee, a season of good news to all those who are humble. During this jubilee, every debt is cancelled, all that was lost is restored, and slaves are released from bondage. Jesus came to proclaim that He is that jubilee for every man that would believe in Him. He is bestowed with power to mend broken hearts, free captives, and open prison doors for those who are bound. His mission is twofold in nature.

First, because of His sacrifice, He brings comfort and restoration to all who mourn because of the desolation and grief experienced in their lives. Secondly, from these restored vessels, He establishes a new anointed priesthood to help administer God's jubilee. Upon these ministers, He bestows an appointment of beauty, joy, and praise, by the baptism of the Holy Ghost and fire, so that they might rebuild the old waste places, raise the former desolations, and repair the waste cities of many generations. God's heart is to lift every life from the charred ash heap of despair, turn them around, flood them with joy and gladness, and strengthen them with praise and thanksgiving.

It is God's intention to give every man and woman the opportunity to dwell once again in safe places, in restful places, in truthful places, in grace, and in perpetual fellowship with Him. He wants to establish His Garden of Eden in and around you.

The restoration of the broken relationship with God and the loss of man's glory covering in the garden was once and for all secured by Jesus. It is the answer to every man's question of, "Why are these things happening to me?" For God so loved the world, that He gave His only Son that whosoever believes in Him, will not perish, but have everlasting life.

Maybe you haven't experienced the wonderful saving grace of God in your life. If that is the case, it is easy to do. Simply say, "Lord, forgive me of my sins. I turn from my anger, bitterness, hurt, and rebellion so that I may follow You. Come fill my heart with Your presence and baptize me with Your Holy Spirit and fire. Amen!"

NOTES

What Every Man Needs to Know

NOTES

REFERENCES

Access your bible from anywhere (1993) BibleGateway.com: A searchable online Bible in over 150 versions and 50 languages. Available at: https://www.biblegateway.com/ (Accessed: 15 March 2023)

"Dictionary.com | Meanings & Definitions of English Words." In Dictionary.Com, Mar 7, 2023. https://dictionary.com

"Does Genesis 3 Suggest That Adam and Eve's Fig-Leaf Loincloths (v. 7) Were Unable to Cover Nakedness, Unlike the Tunics of Skin (v. 21)?", hermeneutics.stackexchange.com, August 25, 2021. https://hermeneutics.stackexchange.com/questions/66983/does-genesis-3-suggest-that-adam- and-eves-fig-leaf-loincloths-v-7-were-unable

About the Author,

Reginald Alexander Travis

I am a first-time author with a passion for writing and communicating with people. I was trained in architecture and design at Virginia Tech University. For the past thirty years, I have worked as a lead designer for the Volvo Truck Corporation. I am happily married to my beautiful wife, Charlene, and we have four children. We reside in Blacksburg, Virginia, where we attend a local church in the area (Christian Growth Center), where my wife and I serve as elders. In addition, I have had the honor of leading praise and worship for that body of believers for several years. We are grateful to have received a solid foundation of biblical principles and grace while helping to build God's kingdom and spread the love of Jesus Christ.

Printed in the USA
CPSIA information can be obtained
at www.ICGtesting.com
CBHW050945210724
11802CB00023B/461